RED GUIDE

North Cornwall

Newquay Perranporth
Padstow Tintagel
Bude, etc.

Edited by Reginald J. W. Hammond

Nineteenth edition

WARD LOCK LIMITED

116 BAKER STREET, LONDON, W.1
and at Sydney

Maps and Plans

This Guide covers the north Cornish coast from St. Agnes to Morwenstow, and includes the resorts of Newquay and Bude.

© 1971 **Ward** Lock Limited ISBN 0 7063 5417 6

Colour illustrations by courtesy of J. Salmon Ltd., Sevenoaks

Printed in Great Britain by
Cox & Wyman Limited, London, Fakenham and Reading

Contents

BUDE

Illustrations

Introduction

Surrounded by sea on three sides and almost completely severed from the rest of England on the fourth by the River Tamar, Cornwall is very nearly an island and quite different in scenery, customs and climate from any other part of the country. The North Coast, in particular, is a land of legend, of mystery, of romance. For millions of years it has been defended against the raging Atlantic Ocean by the finest stretch of cliff scenery to be found in the British Isles. The man-made attractions of the orthodox seaside resort fade into insignificance when compared with the brilliant colours of the water, the scenic grandeur of the towering cliffs and the natural beauty of the sandy porths which breach them at frequent intervals. This fascinating area can be reached in comfort in a day by express train or coach from London or the Midlands, with bus connections to the more remote parts, while those who make the journey by car are assured of well-surfaced, fast roads to all the more popular resorts. Throughout the North Coast area there are excellent hotels and guest-houses. Accommodation can also be had at inns and farm-houses, and furnished bungalows may be rented. Early booking is, however, essential.

For Road Routes *see* pp. 7–9.

RAILWAY ROUTES

Of the resorts on the North Cornwall coast, only Newquay has direct railway connection. For all other places it is necessary to travel to Truro, Bodmin Road or Okehampton and complete the journey by road services.

Certain services may be subject to alteration and travel facilities should always be verified by current timetables and announcements.

TO NEWQUAY

By train to Par or Bodmin Road and change into the branch connection. On Saturdays during the Summer period excellent through services run between Newquay and London, Birmingham, Wolverhampton, Manchester and Newcastle. Refreshments are available on a number of trains.

TO BUDE

By rail to Okehampton, then by bus.

TO BOSCASTLE AND TINTAGEL

By rail to Bodmin Road or Okehampton, then by bus.

TO PADSTOW

By train to Bodmin Road, then by bus.

TO PERRANPORTH

Passengers travel by train to Truro or Redruth then by bus.

MOTORAIL SERVICE

British Rail's Motorail Service runs from Kensington Olympia to St. Austell conveying cars and up to four adult passengers at an inclusive charge including reserved accommodation for the car party.

COACH AND BUS SERVICES

A popular way of reaching Newquay and district is by long-distance passenger coach from London and main provincial centres. The fares are less than those charged by rail and travellers are sure of a seat. The journey, however, takes longer, personal luggage is restricted and seats at week-ends must be booked well in advance. The journey from London takes approximately twelve hours. Particulars can be obtained from Victoria Coach Station, Buckingham Palace Road,

London, S.W.1 (Tel. 01 730 0202), or from Main Coach Stations in the provinces.

Cornwall is very well served with buses. Routes radiate to all parts of the Duchy from Newquay. The great majority of the services are controlled by the Western National Company (whose local agents, or the railway, will supply time-tables, etc.), but there are still a few private-enterprise companies operating local services connecting small towns and villages. Particulars of the latter can generally be obtained from the village post office or the local inn.

ROAD ROUTES TO THE WEST

Two excellent roads lead into Cornwall and serve the resorts described in this Guide. The more famous is—

THE LAND'S END ROAD (A 30)

which leaves London by way of Hammersmith and the Great West Road, and continues by Staines and Basingstoke (by-pass) to **Salisbury** (82 miles from London). (The alternative A 303 after Basingstoke, branching right for Andover and Amesbury, etc., provides a quick through route to Exeter.) Entering the beautiful old city of Salisbury, turn, on the right, along St. Mark's Road (2nd turning after St. Mark's Church). Turn right then left at the end into Wyndham Road. Right at the end again, into Castle Street, under railway bridge then sharp left, right through into St. Paul's Road whence across at the end into Wilton Road and so in 20 miles to **Shaftesbury.**

Shaftesbury is entered by Salisbury Street, which becomes High Street, bears round to the left and in 200 yards bears away to the right. Avoid turns to left and right, but at a fork take the left-hand road (New Road); in about a quarter of a mile turn sharp to the left, a quarter of a mile farther keep again to the left, on the Sherborne and Yeovil road. At 125 miles **Yeovil** is entered by way of Sherborne Road. Keep left at the fork (right leads to Taunton in 26 miles) and bear left again at next fork. Follow up South Street as far as traffic lights (halt sign after dark), where turn left for Honiton and **Exeter** (169 miles).

Exeter is entered by Paris Street. At the roundabout turn

7

left, continuing along the Inner By-Pass to Exe Bridge and on the south bank enter Cowick Street, and so out on to the **Okehampton** Road (A30). The Exeter by-pass, of course, makes it possible to avoid the city in a wide detour. This leaves the road from Honiton two miles after Clyst Honiton and goes southward *via* Countess Wear, rejoining the Okehampton road by way of Alphington (A 379) and Cowick Lane.

Those bound for **Bude** (222 miles from London) turn north at Okehampton: the road is *via* **Holsworthy** and **Stratton,** where turn left and almost immediately to the right, and again to the right after climbing the short winding hill.

For places farther down the coast it is better to keep to the main road from Okehampton and on to **Launceston,** at the top of a steep hill, 212 miles from London. About 5 miles beyond the town, branch right for **Boscastle** and **Tintagel** and the north coast *via* Camelford, but the main road crosses the open Moor, dropping steeply into **Bodmin.** By Fore Street and Lower Bore Street go to the west end of the town, branch right for Padstow, Wadebridge, Polzeath and Rock at the clock tower—straight on for all towns to the west. After 12 miles turn right at Indian Queen for **Newquay,** including Watergate Bay, Mawgan Porth, Porth, Crantock and Holywell Bay. For **Perranporth,** however, keep to the main road from Indian Queen until, at Zelah cross-roads, a turning on the right leads down to Perranporth in about 3 miles.

From Bristol and the Midlands motorists join this road at Exeter, and their route is either through the crowded city by Sidwell Street, High Street and Fore Street, or preferably by the Inner by-pass and over the bridge as above; unless they avoid the city by taking the Exeter by-pass at the A.A. box three-quarters of a mile after passing through Pinhoe.

THE ROUTE VIA BIDEFORD

Those whose destination is in the neighbourhood of Bude, or who wish for an alternative to the much-used Land's End road, should take the Barnstaple road from **Taunton** (143 miles from London by way of Basingstoke, Amesbury, and Wincanton). Either by-pass Taunton entirely by taking a road to

8

the right marked Minehead and Barnstaple just before reaching the town, or, in Taunton bear to the right and follow North Street and Bridge Street, the main thoroughfares, and then bear round to the left by Staplegrove Road (for Barnstaple). There is now a good clear run to **Wiveliscombe** (where turn to the right and ascend very steeply, turning to the left at the top) and on to **Bampton.** Hence to **South Molton** and **Barnstaple,** which is entered by Taw Vale Parade. Cross the Bridge, shortly ascend to the right and follow road to **Bideford.** Cross the bridge, turn sharp to left at far end, and in about 200 yards turn sharp to the right, up Torridge Hill. Take first turn on left, and just past infirmary buildings go to left again. The road is now clear for 10 miles to **Clovelly Cross** (the village lies below, to the right). Here turn left for **Stratton,** where turn right for **Bude,** about 228 miles from London.

For Camelford, Tintagel, Boscastle, Wadebridge, Newquay, and places farther south, keep straight ahead in Stratton. For directions to other places in the district see the chapter on Motoring, p. 147.

ACCOMMODATION

North Cornwall is well provided with hotels, large and small, and there are numerous guest and boarding-houses. In addition there is a wide selection of farm-house accommodation. Throughout this Guide is given a representative list of establishments in the various resorts. Full lists of all types of accommodation can generally be obtained on inquiry to the local authority concerned. In all cases booking must be made well in advance.

THE RED GUIDES

Aberystwyth
Anglesey and North Wales

Barmouth, Harlech, etc.
Bournemouth and District
Broads and Norfolk Coast

Channel Islands
Cornwall: North
Cornwall: South
Cornwall: West
Cotswolds

Devon: South
Dorset Coast

Exmoor and Doone Country

Infracombe and N.W. Devon
Isle of Man
Isle of Wight

Lake District
Llandudno, Colwyn Bay
London
Lyme Regis and District
Lynton and Lynmouth

New Forest

Peak District
Penzance and W. Cornwall

St. Ives and W. Cornwall

Tenby and South Wales
Torbay and South Devon

Wales, N. (Northern Section)
Wales, N. (Southern Section)
Wales, South
Wye Valley

Yorkshire Dales

SCOTLAND

Aberdeen, Deeside, etc.
Edinburgh and District
Highlands
Inverness, Strathpeffer, etc.

Northern Scotland
Oban, Fort William, etc.
Western Scotland

RED TOURIST GUIDES

Lake District (Baddeley)
Complete Scotland
Complete Ireland

Complete Wales
Britain

Portugal (Sarah Bradford)

Japan (William Duncan)

WARD LOCK LIMITED

North Cornwall

Cornish Scenery—Place Names—Walking—Golf—Sea-
Fishing—Camping—Climate—Natural History
—Geological Note—Ferns

The part of Cornwall dealt with in this Guide extends, south-
wards, along the coast from the North Devon border at
Marsland Mouth to St. Ives; north of the main road from
Launceston, through Bodmin, to the west. Within this area
lies a wealth of magnificent scenery; relics of prehistoric
civilisation, medieval churches, ancient castles, crosses and holy
wells; legends of piskies and "knockers"—all bounded by the
indomitable granite cliffs, against which the mighty Atlantic
whispers or thunders, according to its mood. Those who decide
to explore this territory thoroughly will have solved the holiday
problem for several years ahead, and moreover, with an occasional expedition into the adjacent country, they will have
opportunities for acquiring a full knowledge of Cornwall as a
whole—the nature of the land and the characteristics and
activities of the people.

One of the most remarkable facts about the "Delectable
Duchy" is the *variety* of its scenery. Not only does the North
Coast differ from the South (both in climate and in scenery),
but each cove, each fishing port, each town and each holiday
resort is completely different from the last. The climate of the
North Coast is fresh, invigorating and equable. As compared
with the South, the scenery is wilder and more rugged; nature's
colouring more brilliant. The high ground and the clean and
clear atmosphere afford panoramic views over great distances
of land and sea; steep hills and deep, wooded valleys alternate
in confusing sequence, decorated with bright splashes of colour
from gorse and heather. From the Hayle estuary to a mile or so

north of Gwithian; for a few miles north of Perranporth and again at Bude, there are breaks in the cliff wall and here are the Towans (sand hills) bound with long, tough grass, which great gales have piled up over the centuries.

For the benefit of holiday-makers who wish mostly for quietude, rest, and perhaps solitude, in conjunction with beautiful scenery, fresh air, and daily creature comforts, it should be mentioned that piers and promenades are dispensed with, as are the "amusements" common to most popular holiday resorts. In fact, after a year's toil in the hive of life there is no more efficacious recreation than to spend a quiet, healthy holiday among the bastioned crags of the North Coast of Cornwall.

Cornwall is peopled by a hardy and independent race, whose Celtic ancestors toiled and lived close to nature, mostly as fishermen or miners. They are a courteous and hospitable people, always quick to appreciate and return a kindness. In early days they traded their tin and copper with visiting maritime nations from the Phoenicians onwards, during which time they absorbed Spanish and Breton blood and traditions, and, in the early days of Christianity, welcomed missionary saints from Ireland and Wales. It is small wonder that dark and alien types persist among the hospitable countryfolk, that belief in drolls and piskies is inherent, that religious emotion is fervent, and that over the whole country a faint but delightful foreign flavour is apparent.

This can only be due to factors of race and history, and cannot be attributed to language, for with the exception of distinctive place-names and surnames, the Cornish branch of the Celtic language has been dead for several centuries, and any revival of it could be of academic interest only.

> "By Tre, Pol and Pen,
> Ye shall know Cornish men."

Both the names and the mining tradition have persisted through the centuries, and since most of the local mines have closed down, Cornish Tres, Pols and Pens are found on gold-fields and tin-fields all over the world.

Apart from place-names of obvious Cornish origin, many

others sound strange to visitors from "up-country". Here is a very short selection:

	Near		Near
Barkla's Shop	St. Agnes	*Promised Land*	St. Agnes
Bugle	Roche	*Rose*	Perranporth
Come-to-Good	Devoran	*Turn-a-Penny*	Kea
Crumplehorn	Polperro	*Twelveheads*	Bissoe
Goon Gumpas	St. Day	*Ventongimps*	St. Allen
Gilley Gabben	Gweek	*Voguebeloth*	Redruth
London Apprentice	St. Austell	*Washaway*	Wadebridge
No-Man's-Land	Wadebridge	*Woodsaws*	Lanreath
Polly Joke	Newquay	*Yondertown*	Roche

To those curious as to the meaning of Cornish place-names it may be instructive to know that:

Als, Alt, is a cliff	*Maen*, a stone
Bal, a mine	*Nans*, a valley
Bos or *Chy*, a dwelling	*Pen*, a headland
Bryn, a mound	*Pol*, a pool
Car, a fort	*Porth*, a port or cove
Carn, a heap of rocks	*Ros*, a heath
Dinas, a fortification	*Ruan*, a river
Droke, a channel	*Tre*, a town
Eglos, a place of worship	*Tol*, a hole
Fos or *Vose*, a ditch	*Towan*, a sand-hill
Goon, a moor	*Wheal*, a mine or shaft
Lan, an enclosure	*Zawn*, a chasm

The churches are the most interesting and characteristic of the works of man in the county. Dedicated to long-forgotten British saints, some are the centres of closely-built villages sheltering in the combes, while others stand lonely sentinels on the uplands, and serve widely scattered parishes, their tall towers beacons for sailors. A striking similarity is seen in their history. Many were rebuilt or enlarged in the fourteenth and fifteenth centuries; some suffered neglect during the Commonwealth; more were ruined aesthetically though preserved in fabric in the nineteenth century. Now with the awakening of artistic conscience their ancient beauty is being restored. Commonplace pine pews have been replaced by ancient bench-ends or modern ones carved in traditional fashion by local craftsmen; rood-screens painted and gilded in the original colours; ornate disfiguring plaster removed to reveal the simple dignified stonework below.

Walking

Walkers, on account of the steepness and broken character of the coast and the many inland detours necessary, will not be able to cover many miles a day. Nor will they wish to, for almost every turn calls for a pause and admiration. The hotel and inn accommodation is generally all that could be desired. Newquay, Bude, Boscastle, Tintagel, Padstow, St. Agnes, and Perranporth have excellent hotels, but some of the villages lack an inn. Those who intend to attempt the grand but arduous tramp along the North Coast, between Hartland (in Devon) and St. Ives, should remember that it is not only more pleasant to walk *towards* the north-east, with the sun *behind* during the greater part of the day, but the brilliant Cornish colouring is also seen to the best advantage. The same applies, of course, to motoring.

Golf

Bude has a fine eighteen-hole course on Summerleaze Downs, close to the shore, and clubhouse available to non-players. Newquay has a delightfully situated, if difficult, course of eighteen holes, with natural bunkers. Lelant, by St. Ives, has a round of eighteen holes; and the golfer will tire himself long before he has mastered the subtleties and potentialities, as Dr. Johnson would have said, of the magnificent eighteen-hole course of the St. Enodoc Golf Club at Rock, near Padstow. Perranporth has its eighteen-hole course among the dunes and there are courses at Mawgan Porth, at Trevose, Truro, etc. Further particulars of the various courses are given in the descriptions of each centre.

Fishing

The sea-fishing is distinctly good all round the Cornish coast. On the north coast a favourite ground is by the Quies rocks off Trevose Head. Boats and experienced men are always available.

Fresh-water anglers do not usually fish along Cornwall's north coast, for the streams are small. Bude, Boscastle, Tintagel, and Padstow offer the best opportunities. Unfortunately for sport, so many of what would otherwise be fine trout-streams are polluted with washings from china clay works, which give them a milky-white appearance, though this does not apply to the same extent along the north coast.

Camping and Caravanning

The numerous well-wooded and sheltered combes, or *porths* as they are called, running down to the sea, render North Cornwall excellent camping country, and an increasing number of car-drawn caravans are seen each summer. There is rarely difficulty in finding a site, and some of them—at the edge of a sheltered wood looking over golden sands to the sea—are ideal; but motorists with heavy caravans and rather light cars should be very careful when approaching some of these combes, the roads often dropping in gradients of 1 in 5 or 6, and warning notices are not always in evidence.

As we have said, there is rarely difficulty in finding a good site, and as a rule permission to pull in or to pitch camp is readily granted.

A comprehensive list of caravan sites may be obtained from the Cornwall County Council.

Climate

From Bude south-westward the health resorts on the north coast of Cornwall are more invigorating in summer than those on the south, but the difference decreases south-westward, until at St. Ives the variation from Penzance is not nearly so marked. The high and open position of Newquay renders it more suitable for summer, when its bracing air is unexcelled in the West; but there are many sheltered spots near where the mild winter of Cornwall may be thoroughly enjoyed, to the special advantage of those to whom a degree or two, more or less, of temperature is of less importance than protection against the stronger winds.

The rainfall in North Cornwall is less than in South Cornwall. It may be interesting to note that sunset time is 23 minutes later than London. The Summer sea temperature varies between 58 and 61 degrees.

In a normal winter Newquay, in common with most of Cornwall, sees little snow, and frosts are of a mild character.

Tintagel and Boscastle are quiet, restful spots where the bracing Atlantic breezes can be enjoyed to the full while Bude possesses all the best health-giving qualities of the other North Cornwall resorts.

Natural History

Cornwall, generally, is a wonderful place for the naturalist, and the north coast claims its share of rare plants. The variety of habitat

15

provided by headlands, meadows, seashore and inland lanes, downs and moors has given rise to an extensive and interesting flora, while the beaches at Fistral, Bedruthan and Perranporth amply repay collectors of shells.

Of wild life, perhaps the birds are the most prominent features, with, of course, sea-birds first. Of others, sparrow-hawks and kestrels are fairly common, and magpies are numerous. Peregrine falcons are sometimes seen northwards, towards the Devon-Cornwall boundary, as well as the Cornish chough (now very rare indeed), the buzzard, and the raven.

Cornish birds—or birds found in Cornwall—comprise 303 species of which 83 have been classified as residents, 58 as winter visitors, 27 as summer migrants, 70 as casual visitors, and 65 accidental visitors. Cornwall's geographical position accounts for the two latter classes.

Seals are found along the cave-worn coast, more especially at Boscastle, Trevaunance Cove, St. Agnes, and Newquay. At the latter place, Pentire Head and the Gazzle (Towan Head) are favourite haunts.

Badgers and foxes are fairly plentiful.

Geological Note

Geologically, Cornwall is unique among English counties. Built up as it is of ancient sedimentary rocks which have been invaded by acid igneous rocks, the phenomena of alteration by heat and of mineralisation are to be seen in great variety.

The foundation of the county consists of very ancient rocks, which vary from those of Carboniferous age in the north-east, through Devonian rocks in the centre to Pre-Cambrian rocks in the Lizard promontory. These have been invaded by dykes and sills of basic igneous rocks, the Greenstones, during Devonian times, and then, about the close of the Carboniferous period, the whole of the area was invaded by acid molten material which rose from below, lifting the slaty rocks above it, and cooling slowly under a thick cover of sedimentary rocks to form the granite of the West of England. During the consolidation of the granite, solutions containing volatile substances rose through fissures in the rocks, altering the rocks on either side and filling the fissures with metallic and other minerals to form the lodes.

After the formation of the granite, Cornwall was for a long time high land which was weathered away by the action of wind, water, heat and cold, so that the slate cover was partly removed from the top of the granite and the upper parts of its uneven surface were later exposed as granite hills.

Later, Cornwall was depressed and almost wholly submerged in the ocean, while in Pliocene times it was elevated by stages giving rise to gently sloping terraces at altitudes of 1,000 feet; 700 feet; and 400 feet. These form characteristic features of Cornish scenery.

Near Camelford three of these terraces can be seen at altitudes of 1,000 feet, 700 feet, and 400 feet above sea-level. Nearer the sea-level there is a raised beach which marks another stage in the rise of the land and which can be seen at Godrevy, and other points on the north coast. That at Fistral Bay is now covered by sand.

To the petrologist and mineralogist, Cornwall is a happy hunting-ground, so varied and numerous are the rock types and so extensive the series of minerals. Fossils are also to be found to the east of Newquay.

The chief rocks of Cornwall, in order of age are:

Alluvium, peat and "head"	Recent
Raised beaches, stream tin	Pleistocene
Sands, clays and gravels	Pliocene
"Elvans" or porphyries, aplite, pegmatite, mica traps and granite	Permo-Carboniferous
Culm Measures	Carboniferous
Slates, grits, basic dykes and volcanic rocks .	Devonian
Granite, basic dykes, serpentine, hornblende, gneiss and schists of the Lizard . . .	Pre-Cambrian

Cornwall has been subjected to great pressures and stresses in the past, due to earth movements. This has caused the slates to become completely folded and faulted; a phenomenon which is especially well shown in the cliffs at Bude, Porth and Godrevy. During past geological ages the whole county has been subjected to both elevation and depression. In early Pliocene times the high ground emerged from the sea to form a group of islands.

After these movements of elevation there was a depression of the county which resulted in the submerged river estuaries which provide the fine harbours of Falmouth, Fowey, Looe, Plymouth, etc. The depression also submerged forests, remains of which can be seen at Bude, Padstow, and Portreath.

During the glacial period Cornwall did not experience such an arctic climate as the more northern parts of England, but the high ground must have been snow-clad and there are signs that small glaciers were at one time present on Bodmin Moor. When the climate became gradually warmer the melting ice stimulated the flow of the rivers and enabled them to cut the steep-sided narrow valleys which are so characteristic of the north coast.

Localities of Geological Interest

Barras Nose, Tintagel. Basalt with magnetite.

Bedruthan Steps. This part of the coast illustrates the wear and tear due to the action of the sea.

Camelford. The slates round the town show the effects of heating by the granite; spotting and crystals of andalusite.

Castle-an-Dinas. On the north side of the hill—known as Castle Downs —is an old disused wolfram mine.

China Clay. Many pits are to be seen between St. Dennis and St. Austell. The clay rock is washed down by monitors and the clay stream pumped to the surface, where the coarser components are separated in narrow channels, the "mica drags". The clay is then settled in concrete tanks and afterwards dried on a "pan" heated by hot air in flues below. China clay is used not only for porcelain but also in the manufacture of paper, cloth, face powder, etc.

Cligga Head. The cliff can be descended by a path on the south side of the head. Gneisen veins with cassiterite, wolfram, tourmaline, and various micas are to be seen in the cliff.

Crackington Haven. The rocks in the coves are Culm Measures. A thrust plane is seen cutting across the beach. Goniatites in slates.

De Lank Quarries. Granite is worked here, and the cutting and polishing of the stone can be seen.

Devil's Jump (near Michaelstow). A craggy gorge made by a reef of quartz which also appears at Lanlavery Rock near Roughtor.

Delabole Quarry. A quarry in roofing slate nearly 500 feet deep (see p. 80).

Fistral Beach, Newquay. Below the Headland Hotel is a raised beach, covered by cemented blown sand.

Goss Moor. Once the scene of intensive mining for alluvial tin gravels.

Newquay Headland (Towan Head). Dykes of mica trap cut the slates of the headland.

Perranporth. On the Droskyn side veins of cassiterite are to be seen in the slates. The arches are due to old mine workings. At the north end of the sands the Great Perran Iron Lode outcrops.

Port Isaac. Spilite basalt is to be seen in the quarry alongside the lane leading south from the village, also at Pentire Head.

Roche Rock. This outcrop of schorl rock, an altered granite composed of quartz and tourmaline, is part of a wide vein running through china clay rock. The latter, being soft and incoherent, has been worn away, leaving the hard schorl rock as an upstanding mass.

Rock, opposite Padstow. Dykes of Proterobase are to be seen in quarries in the sandhills.

St. Agnes. Pliocene sands occur on the north side of the beacon and there are many lode outcrops in Trevaunance Cove.

Treamble, Perranporth. Iron mine with siderite and limonite.

Trebarwith Strand. Volcanics and chloritic slate with calcite.

Trevose Head. Basic dykes and highly altered slates occur along the shore both north and south of the headland.

Tremorebridge Quarry. (Near Lanivet.) A quarry in granite porphyry shows highly altered slate along each side, with axinite, garnet, and epidote.

Watergate Bay. Splendid cliff sections. Fossils can be found in the slate and an iron lode carrying chalybate occurs.

Widemouth Bay, Bude. Rockfolding.

Cornish Ferns

Nearly all visitors to the Duchy exclaim at the luxuriant ferns flourishing in the hedges with the facility of weeds.

The following is a useful and comprehensive list of ferns found in Cornwall.

COMMON

Brake. Bracken (*Pteridium aquilinum*).—Ternately compound fronds. Very common.

Hard Fern (*Blechnum Spicant*).—Fertile fronds pinnate, covered with brown spore cases in late summer and autumn. Barren fronds taller and green. Never found on chalky soil.

Black Spleenwort (*Asplenium Adiantum-nigrum*).—A one-foot evergreen, with the characteristic linear sori borne obliquely on the upper side of the veinlets. Very common.

Maidenhair Spleenwort or Common Wall Spleenwort (*Asplenium Trichomanes*).—Slender black stalk with deep green fronds. Fruits the whole season.

Lady Fern (*Athyrium Filix-femina*).—Fragile, pale green fronds, lanceolate, and pinnae alternate; pinnules pointed and deeply cut.

Hartstongue (*Phyllitis Scolopendrium*).—Fronds are oblong, tongue-like and simple, with a leather texture and a glossy surface. Stalk is short and shaggy, brown at the base.

Male Fern (*Dryopteris Filix-Mas*).—Bi-pinnate and tufted fronds. Grows in clumps to a height of two or three feet. Pinnules oblong and blunt.

Common Polypody (*Polypodium vulgare*).—Pinnatifid fronds, not tufted, six inches to a foot, oblong to lanceolate. Tangled roots, leathery texture. Slightly unpleasant odour.

Royal or Flowering Fern (*Osmunda regalis*).—Pinnae lanceolate and opposite; upper part of frond thick and brown with clusters of capsules, giving it the appearance of a flower-head. Fruit in late summer or autumn.

RARE

Common Maidenhair (*Adiantum Capillus-Veneris*).—Bipinnate fronds, alternate obovate and wedge-shaped membranaceous pinnules on capillary stalks. A small, delicate and graceful fern.

Wall Rue Spleenwort (*Asplenium Rutamuraria*).—Fronds two to five inches in height, pinnules variable, texture leathery. Stipes as long as the leaf part and dark brownish green.

Scale Fern, Scaly Spleenwort (*Ceterach officinarum*).—Long narrow fronds with rounded lobes, covered with brown scales underneath but a dark green on top.

Brittle Bladder Fern (*Cystoperis fragilis*).—Lanceolate fronds, pinnules deeply indented with serrated edges. Stalk slender, almost black with a few scales at base. Sori at tips of veins of pinnules.

Prickly Shield Fern, Common Prickly Fern (*Polystichum lobatum*).—Bi-pinnate and tufted fronds. Dark green and somewhat shiny, stout and prickly to the touch.

Common Adder's Tongue (*Ophioglossum vulgatum*).—Frond is a pointed green leaf. Stem erect with two lines of capsules. There is a network of veins on the leaf. Resembles the Cuckoo Pint.

The following ferns are also rare:

Tunbridge Filmy Fern (*Hymenophyllum tunbridgense*), Rough Tor, Camelford, in damp woods near Penryn; Wilson's Filmy Fern (*Hymenophyllum Wilsoni*), Rough Tor, Carn Brea; Hudson's Spleenwort (*Asplenium lanceolatum*), very rare in Newquay district, not plentiful except in Penzance district; Sea Spleenwort (*Asplenium marinum*), found in caves in wet places on sea cliffs, e.g. Fern Cavern at Porth, near Newquay; Soft Shield Fern (*Polystichum angulare*), damp shady places in Newquay district; Mountain Buckler Fern (*Dryopteris Oreopteris*), rather rare in East Cornwall, rare in West Cornwall; Narrow Prickly-toothed Fern (*Dryopteris Spinulosa*); Oak Fern (*Thelypteris dryopteris*); Beech Fern (*Thelypteris phegopteris*); Moonwort (*Botrychium Lunaria*).

Newquay

General Information

Banks.—*Lloyds, Barclays, National Westminster* and *Midland*, all in Bank Street.

Bathing.—Excellent at all states of the tide. Extensive sands, clean and firm, but bathers should be cautioned against approaching rocks, especially in Fistral Bay. Bathing at low water on any beach is very unwise. The mouths of fresh-water streams should be avoided at all times. *Cautionary notices are fixed at many spots and should be strictly observed.* Life-guards are employed on the principal beaches, and a flag-warning system operates. On the beaches one may hire deck chairs, bathing huts and beach huts. Surf-boards are available too, for surf-riding is a popular sport.

Beaches.—At Newquay a "beach" is a bay floored with firm golden sand. The largest is Fistral Beach, south-west of the Headland. North-eastward of Towan Headland, and directly below the principal portions of the town, are Towan, Great Western (Bothwicks), Tolcarne, and other beaches, of which the three named are the most popular.

Boating.—Good in the bay in favourable weather. Motor and other boats are on hire in the Harbour. A pleasant hour can be spent on the Trenance Valley boating lake. Sundays all day. Good boating in the river Gannel when the tide serves.

Bowls.—In Trenance Gardens and Eothen Green, Fore Street. Bowls and slips provided.

Buses.—A town service to almost every part of Cornwall. Time-tables are prominently displayed at key points. Western National Bus Station, East Street. (Tel.: Newquay 2322–3).

Car Parks (these arrangements are liable to variation). Fore Street, Crantock Street, Hilgrove Road, Bank Street, and The Whim. Also at the Harbour and Fistral Beach. Many others.

Clubs, etc.—*Rotary Club*, Luncheon meetings, Fridays, 1 p.m. at Golf Club, Tower Road. *British Legion Club*, Gover Lane, billiards, etc., licensed. *Men's Institute* (non-political), Beach Road, billiards, etc. *Belmont*, licensed, Belmont Place, meetings, Tues. and Thurs. *Freemasons' Lodges*, meetings, June–Oct.,

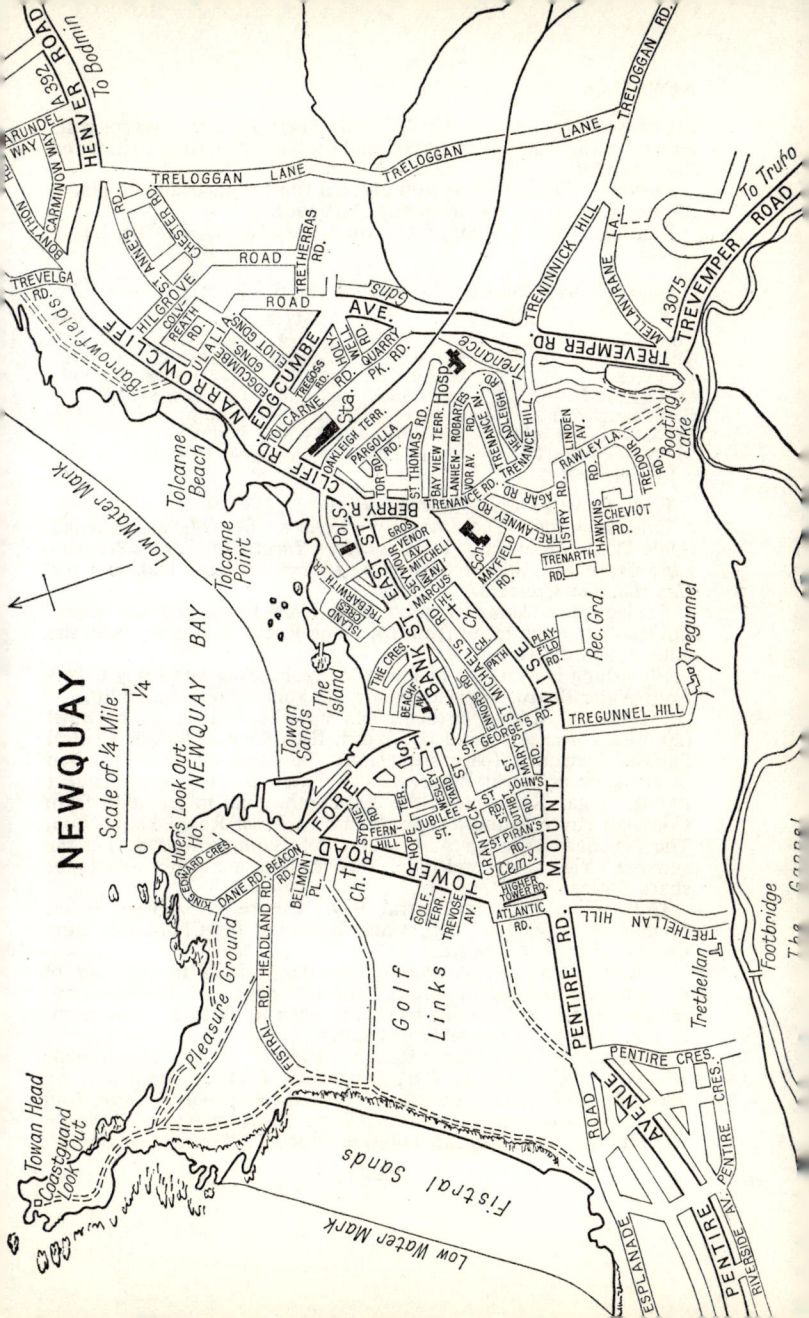

Freemasons' Hall, St. Michael's Road. There are also clubs for golf, tennis, bowls, badminton, cricket and football, admitting visitors for short periods.

Coaches.—During the season coaches run to practically all places of interest near and far, including Dartmoor.

Dancing.—Blue Lagoon, Cliff Road. Also at most of the larger hotels.

Distances by Road from Newquay (Central Square):

	Miles		Miles		Miles
Towan Head	. 1	Holywell Bay	. 4	Perranporth	. 9
The Gannel	. 1	Mawgan	. 5½	Truro	. 16
Crantock	. 4	St. Agnes	. 13	Wadebridge	. 16
St. Columb Porth	. 2	St. Piran's	. 6	Luxulyan Valley	
East Pentire Point	. 1½	Cubert	. 4½	(rail)	. 16½
Porth (or Polly) Joke 3½		Bedruthan Steps	8	Bodmin	. 20
Mawgan Porth (cliff) 5		St. Columb Major	7	London	. 254
(inland road)	. 9				

Early Closing Day.—Wednesday.

Entertainments.—The *Newquay Theatre*, St. Michael's Road (Olde Tyme Music Hall): the *Cosy Nook Theatre* on Towan Promenade; Cinemas: *Astor*, Narrowcliff, *Victoria*, Chapel Hill, and the *Camelot*, The Crescent.

Fishing.—Sea-fishing is good both from boats and the rocks. Lobsters are often taken from the Dane Rocks, and crabs from the holes round the Headland.

Fly-fishing is available in Porth reservoir. Day or weekly tickets from Water Board, Victoria Square, Bodmin, or resident bailiff.

Fresh-water fishing farther afield may be had on river Camel (20 miles), licence from J. H. Ward, Esq., Central Sports, Central Square, Newquay (permission must be obtained from riparian owners), or at Argal Reservoir (25 miles), permit from Resident Bailiff, Argal Reservoir, Near Falmouth. Full information from Cornwall River Authority, St. John's, Western Road, Launceston. The Newquay Angling Association hold competitions during the summer. Visitors are welcome. Full facilities are also available for shark fishing.

Golf.—Fine links on Fistral Bay. Course of eighteen holes. Sunday play. Visitors' tickets may be had at the Club-house from Caddie-Master or Steward.

Temporary Social Membership entitles visitors to full use of Club House and putting-green. The tea-room, bar, bridge-rooms, billiards room and reading-room are open to visitors. Also tennis courts, three hard, available to visitors.

Hotels.—*Atlantic*, Dane Road; *Victoria; Bristol*, Narrowcliff; *Beachcroft*, Cliff Road; *Bay*, Espianade, Pentire; *Grantham; St. Rumon's*, Fistral Bay; *Glendorgal; Headland; Great Western*, Cliff Road; *Penolver*, Narrowcliff; *Edgcumbe*, Narrowcliff; *St. Michael's*, Mount Wise; *Barrowfield*, Hilgrove Road; *Kilbirnie*, Narrowcliff;

Highbury, Island Crescent.; *Trebarwith*, Island Estate; *Beresford*, Narrowcliff; *Savoia*, Lusty Glaze Road; *Pentire; Crescent*, Island Crescent; *Fistral Bay*, Pentire; *Highbury*, Island Crescent; *Beachview*, Island Crescent; *Mount Wise; Min-y-Don*, Island Crescent; *Pentrevah*, Tower Road; *Penruddock*, Tower Road; *Tremont*, Pentire; *Runnymede*, Narrowcliff; *Cotswold;* and many others.

Hunting.—The Fourbarrow (East) Hounds hunt the district.

Information Bureau.—Morfa Hall, Cliff Road. (Tel.: 2716.)

Libraries.— Branch of the County Library, Marcus Hill. Reading Rooms at the Clubs (*see* p. 20).

Licensing Hours.—10.30–3 and 6–10.30. Sundays, 12–2 and 7–10.30.

Motor Routes.—(*See* p. 6.) *For Bodmin, Liskeard, Plymouth, etc.* follow Mount Wise, Berry Road, Cliff Road and Narrowcliff to St. Columb Minor, and thence follow main road.

For St. Columb Major, Wadebridge, etc., fork left just beyond St. Columb Minor.

For Porth, Watergate, Bedruthan, etc., start as above, turning sharp left at the traffic lights.

For Truro, Perranporth and the Land's End Road, take Edgcumbe Avenue, opposite the *Great Western Hotel*, pass under Viaduct and three-quarters of a mile beyond bear right over Trevemper Bridge.

Newspapers.—*Western Morning News* (daily); *West Briton* (weekly). The local papers are *The Cornish Guardian* (weekly); *Evening Herald* (daily).

Places of Worship.—

St. Michael (Parish Church), 8, 10, 11 a.m., 6 p.m., (9 p.m. in summer). Organ recitals, Tuesdays, in summer, 8.15 p.m.

Baptist (*Strict*), *Congregational, Methodist* and *Salvation Army*, 11 a.m., 6 p.m.

Catholic Church of the Most Holy Trinity (summer), 8, 10.30 a.m. and 6 p.m. Extra Services in summer. Weekday mass, 8 a.m.

Days and times of services liable to alteration.

Population.—12,500 (approx).

Post Office.—8.30 a.m. to 6.30 p.m.; Sundays, 9–10.30 a.m. Head Office in East Street, with a Sub-Office at each end of the town, and at Pentire.

Putting Greens at Killacourt, Barrowfields, East and at Trenance Gardens.

Railway Facilities.—Cheap daily return tickets are issued to various points of interest. Inquiries concerning combined rail and road excursions, Run About Tickets and River Fal trips by rail and boat should be made at Newquay station, which is centrally situated at Cliff Road (Tel.: Newquay 2442). *See* also pp. 5–6.

Regatta.—Early August, according to tide. Harbour Regatta and Aquatic Sports.

Riding.—Horses may be hired from several establishments.

River Trips down the River Fal from Truro daily according to tide returning by train or motor from Falmouth, or vice versa.

Tennis.—Thirteen hard and grass public lawn tennis courts in the Trenance Gardens, and six at Mount Wise. Hard and grass courts are available at the Newquay Golf Club.

Zoological Gardens.—Trenance Park.

NEWQUAY

is the most considerable centre and easily the most popular holiday resort on the north coast of Cornwall. It is a bright and cheerful town possessing all the ingredients for a healthy, happy and interesting holiday. It lies midway between Bude and Land's End, 281 miles by rail from London, 254 by road, and 14 miles north of Truro. At this point of the coast Towan Head projects north-westward and with Pentire Headland and Trevelgue Head forms two spacious sandy bays. The principal portion of Newquay has been built, in comparatively recent years, along the cliffs overlooking the more easterly of these two bays, and the eastward expansion still goes on; but the town has rapidly taken command of the wide western bay, and has also spread itself over the northern slopes of the ridge of high ground known as Mount Wise. Many of the houses here have excellent views in all directions: northward over Newquay to the Headland and the sea, southward over the luxuriant valley of the Gannel.

Though it cannot boast of any particular historical interest, Newquay was known under the name of *Towan Blystra* many centuries ago. In 1439 Bishop Lacy, of Exeter, granted an indulgence for the construction, repair and maintenance of the harbour. Carew, the Cornish historian, writing in the reign of Queen Elizabeth, mentions "Newe Kaye, a place on the north coast, so called, because in former times the neighbours attempted to supplie the defect of nature by art in making there a Kaye for the rode of shipping".

In former times Newquay was merely a little fishing village, practically unknown except for its catches of pilchards. A century ago its population could hardly have totalled a hundred; in 1871 it had risen to 1,121. The population now numbers over 12,000 with a rateable value of a quarter of a million pounds—a remarkable story of progress when it is remembered that the main industry (pilchard fishing) has departed, and that the town depends almost entirely on its visitors.

The railway which put Newquay in touch with the rest of the world dates only from 1875. Once given the opportunity, the public quickly showed their appreciation of Newquay cliff scenery, the charm of its vast sands, and the purity and brilliant colouring of its sea, gracious and lovely in fine weather, and magnificent when the wind blows hard from the west and north, or when the ground seas from the Atlantic sweep in line upon line and hurl themselves against the stern, wild cliffs.

Whether by car, coach or bus, visitors will find Newquay one of the best motoring centres in Cornwall. It is well placed for drives to all parts of the Duchy, the roads are good, the town boasts efficient garages, and there is a good network of public road services serving all places of interest.

Here, then, is a holiday playground ready-made by Nature. No man-made pier in the kingdom can compare in grandeur with Newquay's natural pier, Towan Head, which runs for nearly a mile out to sea, covered with soft, springy turf and gay with thrift and other sea flowers. The extremity is a chaos of rocks against which the waves of the Atlantic hurl themselves with stupendous power—in rough weather a sight to be remembered.

From this point the sweep of the coast-line can be followed round, the sheer perpendicular cliffs and rocks showing more or less prominently above the belts of yellow sand, north-eastward past Porth and Watergate Bay to the famous Bedruthan Steps (huge detached rocks nearly 200 feet high), to Park Head, and on till Trevose Head, with its lighthouse, limits the vision.

On either side of the Headland is a fine bay, that to the east being the larger and more populous, though an increasing number of visitors favour the more open Fistral Bay, west of the Headland. Reference to our town plan will show at once how the eastern bay is itself embayed by a series of sandy coves. Newquay can offer shelter from almost any wind that blows, unless it comes from the north-east. When the wind is from

25

the south-west, the various beaches at the foot of the town are in complete shelter, Fistral Bay being somewhat less protected. From a westerly wind the Towan, Great Western and other beaches are sheltered by the Headland, and when the wind is from the east, shelter is to be found in Fistral Bay and on Tolcarne and Great Western Beaches.

At first sight the town appears to consist of a long, winding and busy street close to the edge of the cliffs, with houses and shops on each side. Between the buildings occasional glimpses of the sea can be obtained, and by turning out of the main street terraces and slopes facing the beaches can be reached in a minute. It must be admitted, however, that owing to the lack of foresight of the early builders, Newquay lacks the fine front it might have had. Large numbers of new houses have risen in recent years on the higher ground away from the cliffs, and though these are farther from the sea they have a remarkable range of coast views. The town has also extended downwards towards the Trenance Valley, and on the other side of the golf links towards East Pentire Point, while eastwards it is difficult to see where Newquay ends and Porth begins. The most prominent building in the town is the 'Church of St. Michael, (1909–11), well situated on the slope of Mount Wise. It was designed by Sir Ninian Comper after the style of the old Cornish churches. The new tower (105 ft. high) of the Church was designed by his son, J. Sebastian Comper. The Methodist Church, overlooking East Street, is another building commanding attention, and at the top of the Crescent, in Bank Street, is the rebuilt Congregational Church. There are Comprehensive, Primary, Infants and Nursery schools.

Entertainments

The **Newquay Theatre,** presenting an Olde Tyme Music Hall programme, is in St. Michael's Road. On Towan Promenade is the **Cosy Nook Theatre,** with summer revues. There are **three cinemas** and **dancing** takes place at the Blue Lagoon and also at the main hotels nightly during the season, some possessing their own dance bands.

Tennis facilities are good—hard courts in the Public Gardens at Trenance, and at Newquay Golf Club. There are bowling greens at Trenance Gardens and Fore Street, and putting greens at Killacourt and Barrowfields. Billiards at The Institute, Beach Road, British Legion Club, Gover Lane, and the Belmont Club, Belmont Place.

Bathing Beaches

A glance at the plan will show that Newquay's eastern bay is lined with a series of smaller bays. These are floored with firm sand and are ideal for bathing. Immediately east of the Harbour and overlooked by the Camelot Cinema is **Towan Beach.**

Here the pleasures of bathing may be enjoyed at all times and seasons. The water is delightfully clear, and the far-reaching Headland ensures immunity from west or north-westerly winds or swells. There are bathing chalets available for hire in Tolcarne, Lusty Glaze and Towan beaches. The Harbour is a favourite bathing place at high tide, as diving can be practised from the quays.

North-eastward of Towan Beach is the **Great Western,** or **Bothwicks Beach,** which can be reached at low tide by going round the **Island.** There are good changing facilities. At high tide access to this beach is obtained by the winding road by the Great Western Hotel.

The next beach north-eastward again is the **Tolcarne Beach.** This is reached from the others at low tide, by steps from Narrowcliff at high water and by a cliff path at Crigga Head.

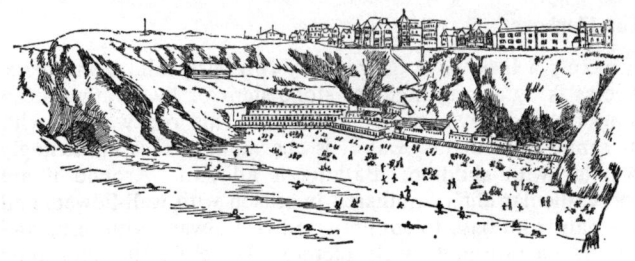

Here again is a plentiful supply of huts. **Crigga** and **Lusty Glaze Beaches** are still farther on, and can easily be reached at low water. From the latter there is a path to the top, coming out on the road to Glendorgal and Porth. *In all cases the tide must be watched, especially when caverns are being explored.* Beyond Lusty Glaze are **Porth, Whipsiderry** and **Watergate** Beaches.

Westward of the Headland is **Fistral Bay** (*see* p. 31), with a splendid stretch of sands. With the golf links at the back and splendid views of the Towan Headland and Pentire to north and west respectively, it is not surprising that this western bay is becoming more popular every year, though extreme care is necessary when bathing.

The Golf Links

are finely situated between Towan Headland and East Pentire, overlooking Fistral Bay and commanding a magnificent all-round view. This 6,000 yards' course of eighteen holes is considered one of the best and most sporting in the county. The hazards and bunkers are formed chiefly by sand-dunes, pits, and stone walls.

The Club-house is the castellated building known as **The Tower.** The entrance is in Tower Road. There is also a pavilion, with verandahs, adjoining the first tee. Large numbers of temporary members including non-players join the Club annually. The Club also has hard tennis courts available to visitors.

The Harbour

is merely a little cove guarded by two very solid stone piers. Access is by a long flight of stone steps or by a rather steep road leading down to the harbour. This rocky inlet, with its sandy floor at low water, is charming, and is increasingly popular with children. Bathing is allowed. Around it are perpendicular cliffs smothered in season with wall-flowers and valerian from base to summit, and rich always with ferns and flowers—a rare and lovely picture. There are the occasional fishing boats (bearing the distinctive **PW** of **Padstow**, the port of registration), but principally yachts, and motor and rowing boats, the majority of which are available for hire.

To reach the North Quay, continue northwards along Fore Street until North Quay Hill is reached on right. A few yards down the hill are seats from which a grand panoramic view of Newquay's magnificent beaches is obtained, with the busy little harbour just below. There are promenades farther down and the quay itself may be reached, either by a steep, rough and narrow lane or by stone steps. Immediately over the Harbour is one of the many shelters and promenades with seats, pleasant for reading and sea-gazing, whatever the weather.

The site was formerly occupied by some pilchard curing-houses known as *Active Cellars*. Formerly the takes of pilchards were enormous, but now the fish seldom get so far up the coast as New-quay, and if they did there are no seine nets with which to catch them. At these cellars the pilchards were salted and pressed beneath large stone weights, and the oil extracted.

The arrival of the shoals was signalled from the **Huer's House**, on the Headland. This little building has great interest for visitors as a symbol of a departed industry, though it is not so old as it looks. To reach it, go along Beacon Road, beside the *Red Lion*, and turn to the right along King Edward Crescent. Thence follow road round to left, keeping well below the *Atlantic Hotel*.

For weeks the look-out man, or huer,* would scan the sea from his stone hut. When once the "cry was up," work of every kind was left, in order that the shoal of pilchards should be secured. It is on record that if the warning was given on a Sunday during divine service, the places of worship would quickly be emptied. On one occasion, October 13, 1835, the cry was raised while a funeral was taking place at Crantock. The body was about to be lowered into the grave, but the people would not wait, and sexton and parson were left to finish the interment as best they could. That night a terrific gale sprang up, and one of the boats was swamped and four hands were drowned.

* Huer (Fr.)—To shout after, to hoot at.

In 1863 was made the largest catch of fish ever known on the north coast of Cornwall. The fish were sighted on October 17 and so thick were they that people were at first incredulous. The pilchards literally filled the bay from Trevelgue Head to Towan Head. The takings of the seine companies that week amounted to £20,000, and 1,000 fish carts came to the town from all parts of the country. The movements of the boats in pursuit of the shoals were directed by look-out men on the Headland and at other points of vantage, such as the Barrows and Trevelgue Head. It is now many a long day since the huer raised his cry at Newquay. The Huer's House, with lovely views along the coast, provides a welcome shelter if caught near the Headland during a shower.

Following the coast towards the Headland, the **War Memorial** comes into sight, and then—

Towan Headland,

or rather the final portion of it, for the Headland actually begins at Towan Beach on the north-east, and West Newquay on the Fistral side. The end portion is really an island, for just beyond the old Lifeboat House, a cutting has been made through the cliff from bay to bay. The highest part of the Headland is the extreme end, where the waves make fine play over the rocks at the base. People gather here, in season and out, to watch the magnificent sunsets for which this coast is famous, and the play of the ever-restless waves. There are seats and a shelter from which delightful views are gained. Those parts of the promontory not built upon have been secured by the town authorities on lease—a step the wisdom of which will be obvious to anyone looking southward from the extreme point of the Head.

Just beyond the old Lifeboat House, on the west side of the Headland, will be noticed, at low water, huge blocks of worked stone and the remains of a pier wall, all that is left of an attempt, years ago, to build a harbour. Close by, under the rocks will be seen the cutting, already mentioned, which separates the extreme point of the Headland.

Beneath the Headland, but now no longer accessible, is a series of caves generally known as the *Tea Caverns*. Here tea was stored by smugglers in years gone by to evade Customs men.

Fistral Bay,

to the more westerly side of the Headland, has a splendid expanse of clean, firm sand when the tide is out.

Lifeguards patrol this beach, but bathing is perfectly safe provided reasonable precautions are taken and foolish risks avoided. The sea at Newquay is the Atlantic Ocean and should be treated with respect, especially at low water, when it is rough, or when there is a strong ground sea running. One should never bathe near rocks or headlands. There is a flag warning system in operation: Red Flag means "Danger" Yellow Flag means "Extra care necessary". The advice of Lifeguards and beach attendants should always be accepted. The Atlantic rollers at Fistral are excellent for surf-riding, and surf-boards can be hired at a nominal fee. This sport is very popular, even with non-swimmers.

Here may be seen how the sand encroaches on the land. Once the golf links were on the top of a low cliff, while the **Raised Beach,** a hard conglomerate of sand and pebbles, which used

31

to be a prominent feature of this coast, is now hidden from sight under a covering of blown sand.

The promontory in the distance, across Fistral Bay, is—

East Pentire Point

The large detached rock close to the Point is the *Goose Rock*. A cliff pathway extends round Fistral Bay, from the Life-boat House, skirting the golf links and joining the Esplanade Road which is a continuation of Mount Wise. The turf-covered Point, or **Pentire Headland,** as it is properly called, is a place to be visited. The Newquay Council have bought it and so preserved it for public use. The views are magnificent.

That end of Pentire Point adjoining the golf links is fast developing into a popular suburb with a number of admirably situated hotels, and buses connect the Point with town and railway station. In spite of development however, two historic tumuli are preserved at the end of Pentire Avenue.

These Pentire Points, east and west of the Gannel estuary must not be confused with the more massive Pentire Point guarding the entrance to the Camel at Padstow twenty miles farther up the coast.

Cliffs and Caves

Newquay may have no "Front" in the ordinary sense of that word, but a walk along the firm sands north-eastwards from the Harbour affords a splendid view of the fine cliffs upon which the town has grown. Tall and precipitous, deeply indented, and pierced with caverns, these frowning walls should be seen when the sun gleams on the sand at their feet, and again—from such a point as the Harbour—when the wind-whipped waves dash in fury about their bases. When the tide is out it is possible to walk all the way to Porth. Immediately on setting out attention is claimed by the lofty detached piece of cliff known as **The Island,** joined to the mainland by a light suspension bridge. All around are piles of jagged rocks, and here and there will be seen small wave-worn caves, not specially interesting when compared with the finer examples near by.

Overlooking the Island and Towan Beach is **Killacourt,** with putting greens, and steps down to the Towan Beach. The cave under Tolcarne Head shows some fine colouring. Across the wide beach is the **Bishop's Cave,** at the foot of Crigga Point, with a grand entrance, and a passage called the Creeping Hole through to another cave. From here onwards to Porth the masses of rock are very fine, and appear much more imposing when closely viewed than when seen from the cliffs above.

Above Crigga and bordering Narrowcliff, opposite the Astor Cinema, are the **Barrowfields,** purchased by the town as an open space. Here may be seen some burial grounds or barrows of the Bronze Age (2500–1800 B.C.). Attention is drawn to one well-preserved barrow which is a good example of the entrenched type.

The putting green here is popular.

The Trenance Valley

The Trenance Valley is the most sheltered part of Newquay. Open to the south and west and screened from northerly winds by the high ground on which the town has been built, its lovely **Gardens** are a glorious mass of colour in late spring and summer. It may be reached by the steep Trenance Road, or by Tolcarne Road, Ulalia Road or Edgcumbe Avenue. In this delightful vale Newquay has a second climate, and here invalids can always take needful outdoor exercise or sit enjoying the surroundings. North-east of the fine viaduct which carries the railway over the valley are the sports grounds, with tennis courts, bowling greens, and putting greens, a car park and a large pavilion where teas, etc., are provided. South of the viaduct are beautiful **Public Gardens** (mentioned above) with seats, shelters, shady walks, a stream, and a pleasant **Boating Lake.** Nearby is **Newquay Zoo.** The gardens and lake are a Bird Sanctuary. The broad road between the Viaduct and **Trevemper Bridge** over the **Gannel Estuary** runs beside the old bridge—an interesting memorial of days past.

Excursions from Newquay

A great attraction of Newquay is its convenience as a **centre** for exploring the grand coast scenery north and south, and the many places of interest inland. Most of the following routes are within a radius of 8 miles of the town.

I. TO PORTH AND ST. COLUMB MINOR

Buses to and from Newquay. Distance two miles.
Car Park.—Near beach.
Church.—*St. Columb Minor*, at the Church town, one mile inland.
Tides.—Any ordinary low tide will permit of access to all the caves at Porth; but, of course, a spring tide is best. (Spring tides at new and full moon.)
Tea Gardens and **Cafes** on either side of the Porth.

From Newquay there is a choice of three routes:

(*a*) By *road*. Follow Cliff Road, passing railway station and Narrowcliff Promenade. Turn off on left at the traffic lights at Porth Way about half a mile after Henver Road turns inland.

(*b*) From Narrowcliff Promenade go through the Barrowfields, between the road and the cliff edge, and follow cliff more or less closely by an obvious path, and after passing between houses, keep going and come out above Porth.

(*c*) All the way across the sands. The last little headland before reaching Porth can be surmounted if the tide is coming in. Steps lead up from Lusty Glaze Beach to join the Porth path.

By route (*b*) the scenery is very fine, the footpath over-looking cliffs about 150 feet high. On reaching the porth (i.e. sandy beach or cove) cross to the farther side, whence may be seen Towan Head, beautifully framed by the narrow entrance. Proceed up the rock steps on the farther side of the stream. This leads to a wooden bridge crossing a chasm and connecting with Porth Island. If the tide is coming in, or the stream is full, it may be necessary to go round the head of the porth, and crossing the stream by the road bridge continue by the road and path (at first bend in Watergate Road) to this point. This is the motorist's approach.

From the wooden bridge, there is seen seawards the bold *Norwegian Rock* to which descent can be made and to the caves near by. Right below is the circular rock pool called the *Wishing Well*. On close scrutiny a large quantity of bent pins will be seen therein. To ensure the fulfilment of a wish pins or coins must be dropped from the bridge.

Porth has good claims to be considered as a holiday resort, and those who like a quiet, restful spot with good sands and seas might well give this popular little place a trial. Accommodation is good and rapidly growing. The extreme point of—

Porth Island

is called **Trevelgue Head,** and immediately below are the **Mermaid's Cave** and the **Blowing Hole,** which run through the rock from one side to the other. At low tide the descent on the south side is not difficult. The cave was once used for smuggling. In rough weather, at about half-tide, the water and air in the cave are forced with terrific power through a narrow opening and the water is discharged in a cloud of white spray, so large as easily to be seen from Newquay. A narrow sea-worn cleft runs up into the island, and here the waves make fine play in rough weather. Note should be made of the barrow and ancient fortifications, where worked flints may sometimes be found. In spring the island is covered with beautiful sea-pinks.

For the **Porth Caves,** return over the island, cross the bridge, turn to the left to rock steps leading down to the rocky little beach. The chief cave, the **Banqueting Hall,** lies towards the right from the gorge beneath the bridge, when looking at the Norwegian Rock. It has two entrances, one facing the sea, the other a small hole in the side of the wall of rock. The latter is usually preferred on account of the water that often remains at the larger entrance. This fine dome-shaped cave is about 200 feet long and 60 feet wide and high. There is a third small exit through the roof at the far end. Note especially the magnificent entrance and its colouring.

Continue round the rocks from the larger entrance to the remains of the **Cathedral Cavern,** immediately on the right, and slightly elevated. In 1883 one of the fine pillars from which the cave derives its name was destroyed and a "wall" fell. Lights are necessary to explore this cave as also in another near by, the **Infernal Regions.** Two paths inside the entrance diverge and meet again later.

In the cliffs near by are several caves, each with special features, such as the beautiful **Fern Cavern,** the roof of which is covered with *Asplenium marinum* ferns. It should be noted that it is useless to take any of these ferns, as they will not live away from the sea air and spray. The **Boulder Cavern** contains some huge boulders rounded and smoothed by the sea.

Cross the fine sands of the bay to a large grass-covered detached rock, an islet at half tide, called **Black Humphrey's Rock,** in memory of a smuggler or wrecker who lived in the mine workings, and who used the island as a look-out. This is called **Flory Island** on the map.

The tide should be carefully observed. The high ground is reached (a) by returning to Porth Bridge via the rock steps on the left of the gorge; (b) by steps in the farther corner of the bay called Whipsiderry.

From Porth onwards to Watergate (about 1½ miles) the cliffs are sheer and perpendicular, while the fallen masses of rock are as fine as any on the coast. The grass-covered rocks, the chief of which rears its head almost as high as the cliffs, are called **Zachery's Islands,** and here will be found other caves and natural tunnels. The fine **Phillory Cliffs** are conspicuous by the large barrows on the summit; it is an exhilarating walk on towards Watergate Bay.

St. Columb Minor

To reach St. Columb Minor from the porth, go to the southeast corner of the little bay. Where the main road is gained another road will be noticed which passes under it by a bridge and runs inland. A turning on the left shortly reaches a path leading in less than a mile to St. Columb Minor. The village, fast developing, is between St. Columb Major and Newquay. Motorists can by-pass St. Columb Minor by taking the road which forks left at the Fairpark School.

The point of the view is the **Church** (services, 8, 11, 8, 15), dedicated to St. Columba. It has a notable tower, the second highest in the county. The interior contains thirteenth- and fourteenth-century work with fine beerstone pillars. The font, a copy of Norman work similar to that at Mawgan (*see* p. 43) dates from about 1500. A portable altar discovered in recent years has been incorporated in the Holy Table. On the north wall is a curious slate slab depicting a man with hands crossed on breast and wide balloon knickerbockers on which are the initials "R.E" and a crown, together with the words MORS MEA EST VITA MIHI—My death is life to me. In the church also are a copy of King Charles's Letter and a large Royal Cipher C.R. The Communion plate was given by Francis, second Earl of Godolphin, and bears the date 1750. The registers date from 1560.

The picturesque **Porth Valley** lies beyond St. Columb Minor, and a short distance to the eastward is **Rialton** (the *Reiltone* of Domesday), at one time the summer residence of Prior Vivian, the last Prior of Bodmin. What remains is a beautiful low house, the old Hall being divided into two storeys, but still with decorated wagon-roof. There is a tunnel-vaulted porch on the ground floor. In the courtyard, now a garden, is a small

Holy Well visible from the main road. This house is only occasionally shown to visitors by special favour. At Rialton farm to the south is to be seen, built into the wall of a barn, an inscribed stone of the fifth century. Still farther eastward is **St. Pedyr's Well**, reached through Treloy Farm, and on the south side of the valley, but better reached by motorists by a turning to the left on the Indian Queen road one and a half miles beyond the Quintrel Downs cross-roads, is **Colan.** The road is narrow, steep and rather swampy in bad weather, but clearly marked. The lonely little church, built about 1300, consists of a chancel and nave of five bays, aisle and south transept, south porch and tower. The base of the old rood screen and stairway remain.

From St. Columb return to Newquay may be made by footpath. One path, rapidly becoming a road, leads from the village westward to the main road, which is followed for a short distance in the direction of Newquay, and then Trevenson Road, the left-hand turning at the cross-roads is taken (to Trencreek). In about 300 yards a path will be found on the right leading to the Trenance Valley sports ground, whence Edgcumbe Avenue leads to Cliff Road and Newquay railway station.

II. TO THE GANNEL AND CRANTOCK

Distance.—Newquay to Crantock, by ferry or footbridge, 1½ miles. The nearest *road route* is *via* Trevemper Bridge, a matter of 4 miles or so.

Tide.—The river Gannel can be crossed (see below) by a small plank bridge at half ebb-tide, and the passage continues open until 2½ hours before high water. There is no regular ferry, but the boatmen will generally put people across for a small fee. Otherwise Trevemper Bridge (1¾ miles inland) must be used.

Close to the junction of Higher Tower Road and Mount Wise Road take a lane running down, southward to Trethellan Farm. Enter the Caravan Park on right, pass through the iron gate below the farm buildings and follow the path down to the water-edge. At low tide the water withdraws to the channel spanned by a plank bridge; but at other times one must cross by boat.

Another route to the plank bridge begins by the path left of the hotel named *Penmere,* at the bend in Pentire Crescent, West Newquay (*see* plan). Near the water a stile on the left indicates the path. Keep to the lower edge of the field.

An alternative way is to take the bus to Pentire, walk down

through Fern Pit Gardens and cross by Fern Pit ferry. The ferry runs all day in summer.

On the opposite side of the estuary is the pretty, wooded **Penpol Creek.** Except at lowest ebb it is well to resist temptations to make short cuts, and to cross the creek by the plank bridge at its head. Then ascend a steep lane, bear to the left, and shortly take field path on right. The path rejoins the lane which soon leads to Crantock.

A modern war-time boat, moored in the Gannel, has been converted into a museum and is open to the public.

A pretty alternative route either out or home, the tide being low, is to cross Penpol Creek at its lower end and follow the southern shore of the Gannel as far as a lane running up to Crantock church. At high tide it is generally possible to be ferried between the foot of this lane and the Newquay side of the estuary, whence the town can be reached by bus or by walking along Pentire Headland.

Crantock,

by reason of its proximity to Newquay and its own charms has many visitors. Accommodation is at a premium in the height of the season. It is a place to examine at leisure; note, for instance, a farm building on the left as the village is entered from Penpol: the lintel of its door is formed from an old carved figurehead. The tea gardens at Crantock are popular with Newquay visitors.

The **Church** (St. Carantoc) is the most interesting for miles round. (Sunday Services, 8, 11, 6; 9 p.m. June–Sept. only.)

The saint founded an oratory here in the fifth century. A collegiate church of considerable importance existed for centuries, being re-founded early in the thirteenth century by Bishop Bruere. The choir was reconstructed in 1224 and a tower added. In 1337 Bishop Brantingham called attention to the perilous state of the tower and left money for its completion, but in 1412 it fell upon the nave and reduced it to ruins. Rebuilding was undertaken shortly afterwards.

In the nineteenth century Crantock Church was in a ruinous condition. The Rev. G. M. Parsons came to the village as vicar, and at once set about a restoration. The interior is dark, but as the eye accustoms itself the full beauty of the very fine screen, incorporating portions of the original, can be appreciated. Much of the fourteenth-century parclose screen in the south chapel is also original. Note the modern bench-ends and a number of beautiful stained-glass windows. The font, of native elvan, is inscribed with the date 1474, but is probably of Norman origin, the date commemorating rebuilding after the fall of the tower. It is said that the foundations of the church are Pre-conquest, but the earliest visible features are Norman choir arches. The chancel arch is Early English, as is also the western tower, as high as the belfry. The register of marriages and burials dates from 1559. The silver chalice of the Communion service is dated 1576 on the cover. In the churchyard may be seen a fine specimen of an ancient stone coffin. Under a roof or canopy in the churchyard to the north of the church are the stocks, with a carving of the "last man in Crantock stocks (*circa* 1817)". Near the south porch is a round piece of an ancient Cornish corn mill.

In the village, facing the War Memorial Hall, is the *Well of St. Carantoc*, over which a stone mound has been built.

According to Hunt's *Popular Romances of the West of England*, Crantock is the site of Langarrow, an ancient city of great wealth and importance. It was also a criminal settlement, and the eventual intermarriage of the convicts with the citizens' daughters caused the population to sink to the lowest depths of vice. Legend says the anger of the Lord fell upon them, and a sandstorm was made to blow for three days and nights, which completely blotted out the city and its wicked inhabitants. It is curious that the church of St. Enodoc to the east and St. Piran to the west have been dug out of the sand, so the legend, as far as the sand is concerned, may have some foundation.

From Crantock a pleasant walk or drive leads to **West Pentire,** with hotel, car park, and tea gardens within easy reach of **Porth** or **Polly Joke** (*see* p. 48) and Crantock Beach. Take the lane between the War Memorial Hall and the Old Well, keep to the left, and at the top turn to the right, past some modern houses. The road gives good views across the Gannel to Newquay and westward to Cubert and Penhale.

The Gannel Estuary

is very picturesque, but is often overlooked by Newquay visitors because it is slightly off the beaten track. At low water on the Crantock side it is possible to walk seawards along the sands from the Gannel crossing to the mouth, which is nearly a mile wide,

NEWQUAY, ST AGNES

English Miles

0   1   2   3   4

WARD, LOCK & CO. LIMITED, LONDON

© John Bartholomew & Son Ltd, Edinburgh

guarded on the right and left respectively by East and West Pentire Points. If the tide is flowing instead of ebbing, the water should be carefully noted, as it rises fairly quickly and the sands are sometimes spongy and dangerous. (On no account should attempt be made to wade *across* the estuary until the advice of local boatmen has been sought as to tide, route, condition of sand, and so on.) It is a pleasant walk by this route to Crantock, either by the sands or the field path which follows the coast. Entering Crantock Bay, the views are magnificent. Here the road runs by the side of the stream to the village.

A convenient way of seeing the Gannel is to take bus or the cliff path from Newquay, by the side of the golf links, and continue all the way round Fistral Bay to East Pentire Point. Part of the journey is along the high ground of the promontory, with the sea on one side and the Gannel on the other. Returning, continue up the valley to the old mill, and back to the town by way of the main road, passing Trenance Gardens and the Viaduct.

III. TO TRERICE MANOR AND ST. NEWLYN EAST

Bus to Kestle Mill (1 mile).

Trerice Manor (National Trust), is best visited on the way to St. Newlyn East by going via St. Columb Minor to Quintrel Downs and then a mile farther on, turning off to the right at Kestle Mill. Though dating in part from the fourteenth century Trerice is essentially a sixteenth-century manor house. The dates 1572 and 1578 are virtually the last touches added to the house. The plaster ceilings of the two large apartments are magnificent. They were carried out by Sir John Arundell, Admiral to Queen Elizabeth I. The large hall window contains 576 panes of glass. *The house is open in summer daily except Fri. and Sat. from 2 to 6. Admission fee.*

St. Newlyn East (*The Pheasant Inn*), two miles beyond Trerice, has a good

41

example of one of the larger Cornish parish churches. This fifteenth-century building, dedicated to St. Newlina, a sixth-century missionary, has an interesting Norman font carved with lilies and cats, some fifteenth-century carved oak bench-ends, a well-preserved Royal Arms of Charles I, and a handsome screen and choir stalls added in the restoration of 1883. Of interest outside is the fig tree growing out of the wall some six feet above ground.

IV. TO WATERGATE

Buses from Newquay.
Road Route *via* Porth (see p. 35). Cross head of inlet and follow road running northward, at a short distance from cliff edge. Steep descent to Watergate needs caution.

This is a pleasant walk from Newquay, the distance being about 4 miles. Proceed as to Porth (*see* p. 35), and continue by the cliff path, which affords excellent views. The path descends steeply into **Watergate,** a deep cleft between hills, with several hotels and houses. Here is a magnificent stretch of sand, extending considerably over a mile. The special attraction is the cliff scenery. Watergate is midway between Newquay and Bedruthan Steps, and less than 3 miles from St. Mawgan, one of the gems of North Cornwall's scenery.

The return to Newquay may be made along the sands, to see the great cliffs from below, and to visit the caves mentioned on pp. 36–7; or the excursion may be combined with that to Mawgan and Carnanton Woods, as described in the next route.

V. TO ST. MAWGAN—VALE OF LANHERNE—CAR-NANTON WOODS

From Newquay the route is as in the previous excursion to Watergate, whence take either the very steep hill beside the hotel or the easier road running inland and bearing round to left. This, half a mile after passing the hamlet of Tregurrian, turns sharply to the left, and, as B3276, passes through Trevarrian, and bending to the right descends steeply to **Mawgan Porth** (5 miles). This must be taken with caution owing to the awkward right-hand turn at bottom.

For Mawgan village turn right shortly after leaving Tregurrian (about half a mile) and take the second left-hand turning through Carloggas to St. Mawgan. (The first turning on the left leads direct to St. Mawgan Church—*see* p. 43.)

A circular walk of 16 miles (which may be reduced by using buses) through varied scenery can be made by taking the cliff path to Watergate. Climb the steep hill opposite, and proceed to **Mawgan Porth**; cross the stream and turn at once inland up the **Vale of Lanherne**. In a mile leave the lane and proceed by footpath (right of road) above the stream to St. Mawgan. Visit church and nunnery, and then enter Carnanton Woods through a white gate up the hill from the *Falcon Inn*. Charming valley scenery.

Mawgan Porth, with its high, rocky cliffs, is very popular. Its breakers provide fine sport for surfing. Here the luxuriant Vale of Lanherne opens to the sea and a glorious stretch of sand is available at low tide. Houses, bungalows and caravans can be rented, and on the northern cliff is the *Bedruthan Steps Hotel*. There are several smaller private hotels and guest houses.

St. Mawgan

The village (*Falcon Inn*) is charmingly set among trees. The River Menalhyl runs down the valley, and with the church makes a delightful picture. Mawgan's beauty has a wide reputation, and is popular with artists, as well as with campers and caravanners. Car parking behind Falcon Inn.

St. Mawgan Church (8, 11, 6), with its fine tower and interesting crosses, is one of the most picturesque in the county. St. Mawgan (or Maucan), a disciple of St. Patrick, was converted and baptized in A.D. 447. The nave with its high arches, chancel with hagioscope and north transept are of the thirteenth century, as is also the lower part of the tower. The medieval font, dating from 1100, has a red painted bowl, and stands on modern Devon marble columns. The fine old pulpit dates from 1553, and the beautiful open screen, with delicate painted pillars, though much restored, is of the fifteenth century. The arms of the Arundells are quartered with those of the Carminows. Note also the ancient brasses to Arundells and others with modern explanatory panels, and the good modern glass in some of the ancient windows. The bench-ends date from 1450.

The **Crosses**. The churchyard cross at the top of the steps by the south-west door of the church is fifteenth-century, and that opposite the lych-gate is said to be eighth to twelfth-century. The former belongs to the class known as Gothic lantern crosses. Though more modern, they are much more beautiful than the "wheel," or solid-headed, crosses found throughout Cornwall. This one in particular has admirable figure sculpture, and is the best example of its kind in Cornwall, though time has not been lenient with the carved stonework. The height is 5 feet 6 inches. The churchyard contains a curious wooden memorial (the stern of a boat), on which are painted the names of ten men who were found in a boat, frozen to death, on Tregurrian Beach in 1846.

The **Carmelite Nunnery,** adjoining the church, was the old manor-house of the Arundell family, but it has been greatly enlarged. The

Chapel is open to visitors and public services are held on Sundays (8, 10, 6) and at other times. An "Assumption" by Rubens is shown, and several other works by old masters. Beside the Chapel entrance is a sixth-century four-holed cross, brought from Gwinear. The community, which is a strictly enclosed order, has been here since 1794. They were French nuns who, having fled to and been expelled from Antwerp, found sanctuary in England. The interest in the convent centres round the ancient manor-house, but of course the public can only see the exterior, and of that only the part visible on the way to the chapel, the rule of the order forbidding any admittance to other parts of the grounds or the interior.

From Mawgan there are two beautiful walks, one to Mawgan Porth through the Vale of Lanherne (p. 43) towards the sea, the other through Carnanton Woods, leading farther inland.

Carnanton Woods

Admission.—Free. Visitors must keep strictly to the main drives (as signposted) between the Middle Lodge, at the turning on the Newquay–St. Columb road, and St. Mawgan village.
Open 10 a.m. to sunset.

At St. Mawgan, the entrance to the woods is by the lodge, a hundred yards up the hill from the *Falcon Inn.* Although a huge tract was cleared during the War, the path between the wooded hills is in delightful contrast to the open uplands around. A new road now leads from Pale Corner, *via* Carloggas, through the woods, to First Lodge in the St. Columb Major road. The ferns are indeed magnificent, and the views become ever more charming in the farther depths. From the Middle Lodge it is 2 miles to St. Columb Major, and 6 miles to Newquay (bus services).

St. Mawgan to Bedruthan Steps. Suggestions for walks are almost superfluous in this neighbourhood of fern-clad, winding lanes and pleasant paths.

Mention may, however, be made of an alternative to the coast walk to Bedruthan. Cross the bridge on the north side of St. Mawgan Church, avoid the left-hand turning and climb a very steep lane ahead. At the top five roads meet. That on the left leads to Mawgan Porth; take the next one which leads steeply down, amid overhanging trees, to a stream and then steadily climbs to the disused airfield at St. Eval. Avoid road on the right, leading to R.A.F. Quarters, and in due course reach the coast in the vicinity of the Steps.

VI. TO BEDRUTHAN (*Foreshore not accessible*)

Distance from Newquay, 8 miles northward by cliffs. This involves some arduous walking, though a bus can be taken for part or most of the way. For the walk from St. Mawgan *see* above. Ten miles by road *via* Mawgan Cross.

Motorists are warned that the roads eastward of Bedruthan diverge confusingly, often without signboards. When in doubt, the newcomer should turn towards the coast; where signposting is better.

From Newquay the best route in many ways is that following the coast by Porth, Watergate, and Mawgan Porth. Here, instead of turning inland up the Vale of Lanherne (*see* p. 43), keep to the road which climbs steeply up the hill to the left. The *Bedruthan Steps Hotel* is passed and some cottages, and then the road flattens out and the run is uneventful to the point where there are indications of the approach to the Steps.

Parking accommodation is ample.

Coach Excursions.—During the season there are daily excursions from Newquay to Bedruthan.

Refreshments can be obtained in the season.

Tides.—At new and full moon low water is at 12 noon (Greenwich—not "summer"-time).

The cliffs at **Bedruthan** are high and precipitous, and carpeted with soft grass and luxuriant heather, while from the sandy beach below, the vivid turquoise sea creaming round their feet, rise great rocks, green-capped on grey.

Legend says that the huge detached masses known as **Bedruthan Steps** were stepping-stones for the giant Bedruthan—hence the name. **Queen Bess,** one of the most prominent, is an excellent likeness to the Virgin Queen, when viewed from the right angle. There is another profile rock close by, a higher one, and the face of a woman is seen looking towards the cliffs. There are numerous large waterworn caverns.

A visit to Bedruthan, even though the foreshore is no longer accessible, is not wasted, for the sea makes fine play round the rocks, especially during a south-westerly gale. But artists love Bedruthan best towards sunset, when the rocks assume most glorious colours. On a clear day, too, the view from the cliff extends even to St. Ives, far away in the south-west. The treasures of Bedruthan are not revealed in their entirety to the hurried visitor.

VII. TO CUBERT, HOLYWELL AND THE LOST CHURCH OF ST. PIRAN

Buses from Newquay and Perranporth to Crantock and Cubert. One service from Newquay goes on to Holywell.

Distance from Newquay to Cubert, 4¼ miles. The site of St. Piran church is about 2 miles beyond, in a south-westerly direction.

Refreshments.—There are shops, tea rooms and guest-houses at Cubert and Holywell.

Road Route *via* Trevemper Bridge, taking right-hand turnings about 2 miles farther for Cubert and a left-hand turning on the Cubert road, a half mile short of Cubert, for St. Piran. Cubert can also be reached by a fair road from Crantock.

Cubert

a pretty little village with colour-washed houses, is the objective of a pleasant walk from Newquay, passing several streams, and high ground from which fine views of the surrounding country are obtained.

Cubert is proud of its little Church on the hill, the spire forming a landmark for a great distance. The roof has remnants of wood-carving of the Decorated Period. The font is late Norman and, like others in the country, preserved its ornamentation in troublous times by a covering of plaster, yet it is unique in design. The narrow thirteenth-century tower-arch is exceedingly graceful. There are monuments dated 1669 and 1699. Note the old bench-ends in the pulpit, the wagon roofs, and the recess for a tomb in the south transept. Outside, built in the west wall of the church tower, about 3 feet from the ground, is a rough, irregular "inscribed stone". The inscription runs: CONETOCI, FILITEJERNO MALI. The stone is probably a memorial of one Conetocus, son of Tejernomalus.

The Holy Well is about 2 miles from the church, in a north-westerly direction, and a signboard points the way. From Newquay the nearest and pleasantest way to walk to the Holy Well is by Crantock, leaving the village by the lane between the Memorial Hall and the old well, avoiding a by-lane on the right and presently rejoining the West Pentire road. This is followed as far as the entrance to Treago Farm

(Treago Road). Continue down the Treago Road past the farm buildings, over the bridge, and by the track *up* the hill (not along its foot near the stream towards Polly Joke). Keeping fairly straight with a trend rightwards, and not too near some farms on the left, a stone wall should eventually be met at a corner with another coming up on the right. Here is an iron gate opening into a rabbit warren, and by turning leftwards and down, the beach at Holywell Bay can be reached. The obvious path straight ahead does not lead to the beach, but to the cliffs above the well.

Motorists from Cubert follow the road to the shops at Holywell Bay, where there is a car park.

The Holy Well is in a cave, access to which can be had at low water during neap tides, but during spring tides it may be reached soon after ebbing half-tide. A series of rock basins, like natural holy-water stoups, lead up to the well, which is larger than the rest. For the following interesting note we are indebted to Dr. C. C. Vigurs, of Newquay:

"In my father's younger days, and in the memory of several older inhabitants of Newquay (as they have told me) since dead, a fair was held yearly on Holy Well beach on Holy Thursdays.

"It was the custom on that day for parents to bring any diseased child and to dip it in the well in the proper manner.

"Above the well is a little cave having its entrance divided by a pillar into two unequal parts; the western (left-hand) part is large and not too steep to be climbed; the eastern (right-hand) part is small, very steep, smooth, slippery, and ends below nearly over the well.

"The father climbed with the child into the little cave through the large opening, the mother standing at the foot of the slippery slope. The father let the child slide down the slope, the mother caught it and dipped it in the well."

Faith was strong in those days, for analysts have since shown the water to be without any special efficacy. The situation and appearance of the well, however, account for much of its reputation.

Note the curious pinnacle rock on the beach of **Holywell Bay**. The cleft rock off the head is **Carter's** or **Gull Rock**.

There is a second Holy Well in the neighbourhood—that of Trevornick—which can be reached by crossing a field on the right of the Holywell road just past Trevornick Farm. It lies on the old pilgrims' route from St. Piran to St. Crantock. It stands in a deep cleft and is also accessible from the beach by turning upstream by the path which goes round past the bungalows.

On the coast, half a mile north of the Holy Well, is **Porth** or **Polly Joke,** a picturesque V-shaped beach between the cliffs, fed by a stream. The distance from Newquay is only three and a half miles. The origin of the curious name is obscure, but in Cornish means "Beach of the Jackdaws (chogha)." Close to Porth Joke is the hamlet of **West Pentire,** with cafés, hotel and car park. Proceeding inland by a good road from here, Crantock is soon reached.

St. Piran-in-the-Sands

Admission.—The Oratory is open daily throughout the year. At various times a Trustee attends the Oratory to give a brief description of the history of the three churches named after the Saint. Visitors are asked to contribute towards the upkeep of the Oratory. Inquiries—Vicar of Perranzabuloe, The Vicarage, Penhallow. Tel.: Perranporth 3245. Services in summer, Sundays, 3.30, and Thursdays, 11 a.m.

The objective of this excursion is the remnant of one of the very earliest Christian buildings in this country. It is enclosed in a heavy concrete vault and only a glimpse of the interior can be had when the door is locked, but at all times the excursion is worth making. For many it is an added charm that the remains are somewhat difficult to find even with directions, particularly on a misty day. The church lies in a hollow among the sand dunes, but to assist visitors to locate it a large 30-foot cross has been erected on a nearby sand dune.

Bus may be taken to Cubert or to Goonhavern whence walk past St. Piran's Round, and through Rose hamlet to Gear Gate.

From Cubert.—Take the path across the fields from the corner of the churchyard opposite the tower, turning left almost immediately at the corner of the hedge (*not* continuing along the well-marked path towards road and house). Cross the fields downwards on to a bridle-path coming out close to Trebisken farm. Continue right, past the farm buildings, and take third gate on left leading into corner of a field, avoiding the other gate more to the right at the beginning of an obvious lane. Inside the gate a path leads downwards by the hedge to another bridle-path which crosses the stream in the swampy hollow. The path threads the swamps, often by rotting logs across boggy patches, and comes out in the open beside a fence with the lofty sand-dunes straight ahead. The path can be seen in places, and by striking ahead uphill at an angle from the farther corner of the fence the beaten path should soon be struck; a straight line drawn through St. Cubert church and Trebisken farm will give direction if difficult to find. The broad track seawards marks the site of a former mineral line, which should be crossed almost at right angles. Through a "pass" between dunes a little plateau is reached, and bearing rather to the right a black shaft is seen on skyline. Keep this somewhat to the left. Nearer approach reveals it as a cottage chimney; when the complete building comes into sight the cross marking the site of the second church (*see* p. 56) can be seen to the right. From the cross, if one looks carefully

Fistral Bay, Newquay

Newquay from the Harbour

Bedruthan Steps

westward (i.e. well to the right of the holiday camp across the dunes), the concrete container of the ruins, resembling to some extent an oil tank, can be picked out and is reached by following the white stones. After heavy rains the path from Trebisken Farm is not a comfortable one and it is advisable then to take the road half a mile eastward from Cubert which goes down past Trebellan farm bringing one to the Gear gate. Whence the path is marked by white stones. Ellenglaze, another farm, west of Cubert, offers another alternative to the Trebisken route. For description of the oratory *see* p. 56.

A return to Newquay on foot can be made by an adventurous way, at a short distance from the cliffs, northward to Porth Joke and West Pentire (*see* p. 48).

For the simpler routes from Perranporth, or from the beach, *see* p. 55.

VIII. TO ST. COLUMB MAJOR—CASTLE DOWNS— NINE MAIDENS

St. Columb Major

Bus Services to Wadebridge, Newquay, Padstow, Bodmin, St. Austell, Truro, etc.

Car Park.—Adjacent to Recreation Ground. One-way traffic is in operation in the centre of the town.

Early Closing Day.—Wednesday.

Hotel.—*Red Lion.* A solid, granite-built house with a history. Polkinghorne, the wrestler, a famous champion of Cornwall, was once host of the *Red Lion*: a fact commemorated by a mural monument. The big dining-hall has a minstrels' gallery.

Market Day.—Cattle market every Monday.

Places of Worship.—*Parish Church, Methodist.*

Population.—About 3,000.

Post and Telegraph Office.—Adjoining the hotel.

Railway Station.—St. Columb Road, 2¼ miles.

Road Route from Newquay starts at end of Narrowcliff Promenade. Turning inland, in about a mile take road on left at Fairpark School just past St. Columb Minor, whence road is good and clear to St. Columb Major (about 7 miles).

Until the advent of motor transport St. Columb was a sleepy town—in size hardly more than a village—never having recovered the ground lost by its refusal to let the railway run through it. Now, however, in spite of one-way regulations, its narrow streets become congested during a busy season. From the predominance of slate and grey stone in its buildings St. Columb has a somewhat bleak appearance; but from its lofty situation, only 5 miles from the coast, it overlooks some very attractive country, and the road from Newquay *via* St. Columb Minor is most delightful.

The ancient Cornish hurling game is played here twice a year (Shrove Tuesday and Saturday week following) and shows no signs of decadence. Of particular historical interest is the *St. Columb Green Book* (so called from its binding), preserving the Churchwardens' Accounts from the days of Elizabeth I. In 1593 there is mention of payment of 10s. for a silver ball for the hurling.

The **Church** (dedicated to St. Columba, an Irish saint) has much of interest. It is a handsome building; at one time it was suggested as the cathedral for the revived Cornish See, and much money has within recent years been spent on its restoration and embellishment. The fine tower rises from outside the building, and rests on two arches, with passage beneath. Inside is a copy of Charles I's Letter of Thanks, painted on a large board. Carved bench-ends from former pews have been incorporated into the modern seats. The Arundell chapel contains brasses of John Arundell and family 1545, and Sir John Arundell and family, 1633. Both the south and north porches have upper chambers, or parvises. The nave arches are high, and well proportioned. The chancel has a beautifully carved roof and the modern oak screens are very fine. All the recent carved work was executed locally, and shows that modern craftsmen are worthy successors to their forefathers. The registers date from 1539. The ancient crosses in the churchyard are of great interest, and just outside the main gates will be noticed the quaint *Glebe Cottage*, bearing date 1638. The Old Rectory, now a hotel, is a moated building in wooded grounds. The whole neighbourhood is picturesque and well wooded, and abounds in wild flowers and ferns.

About two and a quarter miles east by south of St. Columb Major, but a mile farther by road is—

Castle-an-Dinas,

the remains of the most important early British encampment in Cornwall. The original plan can still be traced. By their size, the fortifications were evidently of importance. The name has been variously interpreted, but the most likely explanation is that "An dinas", means "the castle"; when the English came they added their meaning, and so we have "Castle-an-Dinas". The hill itself is called **Castle Downs.** The height above sea-level is 703 feet. There are two tumuli within the enclosure. The moors are said to have been the hunting-ground of King Arthur. Henry Jenner suggested that Arthur was born at Castle-an-Dinas and not Tintagel.

The village of **Indian Queen** (known locally as "Queens"), on the Bodmin–Redruth road, a few miles south of St. Columb Major, is said to have gained its curious name from the circumstance that its inn was visited by an "Indian Queen" journeying by coach from Penzance to London, although it has also been suggested that there is some connection with Princess Pocahontas. Past the road to Newquay is a lane and path on the left leading to an interesting amphitheatre, used for religious services for centuries, and recently restored.

Nearly three miles beyond St. Columb on the road to Wadebridge are the **Nine Maidens.** These are upright stones equally spaced against a hedge some 200 yards to the right of, and parallel to, the road. Another stone, standing apart, is called **The Fiddler.** Sir Norman Lockyer considered that these, like Stonehenge, were set up for astronomical observation and date from 1500 B.C. Local legend, however, declares they were once maidens who were turned to stone as a punishment for dancing on the sabbath. This stone avenue, 350 feet in length, is the only one of its kind in Cornwall.

IX. TO ROCHE ROCK

Routes.—By road *via Indian Queen* and the Bodmin road; or *via* St. Columb Minor, by-passing St. Columb Major on the south and joining the road running to the south of Castle Downs, or Castle-an-Dinas (*see* p. 50), or by a secondary road from Indian Queen through St. Dennis.

The village of Roche is reached by a turning southward from the main road at the Victoria Inn, at the Bodmin end of the long stretch during which road and rail run side by side.

Train to Roche station.

This district, about 10 miles due east of Newquay, is in great contrast to St. Columb Minor. Open expanses of bog and rough grass, dotted with old workings and crossed by rough stone walls, extend on all sides, while to the south-east rise the enormous white pyramids of the St. Austell china clay pits.

The **Roche Rocks** rise surprisingly out of the plain, and are surmounted by the picturesque remains of the old chapel of St. Michael and a hermit's cell. The place is well worth visiting from a geologist's point of view, and also as showing another phase of Cornish scenery. The rocks, a hundred feet in height above the surrounding hills, consist of grey sparry quartz mixed with schorl, the latter appearing in innumerable needle-like crystals. (*See also* p. 18.) The chapel perched on the tallest rock was 22 feet 6 inches long by 10 feet 6 inches wide. It is possible to reach the hermit's cell by the vertical iron ladder on the south side and a second ladder ascends to the chapel. Legend has been busy in regard to these rocks and the chapel. One story goes that the chapel was the refuge of Tregeagle, the unfortunate individual who was given the task by the Evil One of dipping dry the Pool of Dozmary with a limpet shell, when hunted by the Black Huntsman and his fiery-eyed pack.

The village of—

Roche,

close to the rocks, has a church (St. Gomonda), rebuilt in 1822 and restored 1890. The very beautiful Norman font is of Pentewan stone. The registers date from 1572. The fifteenth-century tower is 83 feet high.

In the churchyard is an old **cross,** of more than usual interest. It has rude ornamentation on each side of the shaft, and in the head are four little holes. It stands 7 feet 8 inches in height, and it will be noted that the shaft is wider at the top than at the bottom. Another cross will be found in the field in front of the rectory.

In a hollow adjoining a farm, which is reached by a narrow lane crossing the railway on the north of the Bodmin–Truro road, a quarter of a mile from the Victoria Inn and half a mile from Roche station, is a **Holy Well** (St. Gonnet's), once covered with a deep pointed arch of granite. The figure of a saint which stood in a niche in the roof, and the chapel which also stood near by, have disappeared. It is said that before sunrise on Holy Thursday and the two following Thursdays the country folk used to visit the well to invoke the blessing of the saint by an offering of bent pins, thrown into the water.

Large quantities of tin were formerly raised in this parish, but now china clay is the chief industry. The rivers Par and Fal rise in Roche parish.

About 2 miles south of Roche village is **Hensbarrow Beacon,** called by Carew "the Cornish Archbeacon". With an altitude of 1,026 feet and a tumulus on top, it is an outstanding land-mark, and worth the ascent for the wonderful view from the summit.

Perranporth

Access.—From London (Paddington) to **Truro,** and then by bus. The former Newquay–Chacewater branch line is now closed.

Banks.—*Barclays, Lloyds, Midland.* Open Monday to Friday during season. Winter months, Mondays and Thursdays (10–1) only.

Bathing.—Excellent. Firm hard sands extend for about 3 miles at low tide. Danger notice-boards should be heeded. At low tide bathing is unwise, and the vicinity of the cliffs should be avoided. Some of the best surf-bathing in England. A full-time Beach Guard is employed during the summer months and volunteer members of the Perranporth Surf Life Saving Club patrol the beach whenever possible.

Bowls.—In Boscawen Gardens.

Buses.—To Truro, Redruth, Newquay St. Agnes, etc.

Car Parks.—Three available adjoining sands.

Distances.—Newquay, 9; St. Agnes, 4½; St. Piran's Round, 1¾; Cubert, 4; Truro, 9; Perranzabuloe, 2; St. Piran's Lost Church, 2; Crantock, 6.

Early Closing Day.—Wednesday.

Entertainments.—Dances at the Memorial Hall, St. Michael's Hall, etc.; billiards at Men's Institute and Conservative Club.

Excursions.—There are many coach tours to local beauty spots.

Gliding.—At Trevellas Airfield, ½ mile along St. Agnes road. Facilities for private aircraft by prior arrangement.

Golf Links.—18-hole course on the cliffs eastward (*see* p. 54).

Hotels.—*Boscawen; Sully's; Tywarnhayle; Droskyn House; Bay; Perranporth; Atlantic View; Treberran; Poplars.*

Licensing Hours.—10.30–2.30 and 5.30–10.30 (Summer 11). Sundays, 12–2, 7–10.30.

Places of Worship.—*St. Michael's,* 8, 10, 11, 6; *Methodist Chapel,* 11 and 6; *Catholic* (Christ the King), Holy Mass, 9.30, Sundays, and Holy Days.

Population.—Approx. 3,600.

Post Office.—9 a.m. to 5.30 p.m., Wednesdays 9 a.m. to 12.45 p.m.

Putting and Bowls.—Boscawen Gardens, where is a Boating Lake.

Road Route from Newquay *via* Trenance Valley and Trevemper Bridge. The Perranporth road bears right in 1½ miles (A3075). At centre of Goonhavern turn right.

Tennis.—Perranporth Lawn Tennis Club open to visitors. Eight grass courts. Sunday play, from 2 p.m.

Perranporth has long been noted for its fine rock scenery and its magnificent expanse of hard, golden sand. There are many hotels, a large number of boarding- and guest-houses, many shops, and an excellent water supply. The town lies at the point where two lovely valleys open on to a broad expanse of sand—a children's paradise.

At first glance, Perranporth appears strangely to be an odd mixture of the old and the new—with an undeveloped site

here and there. The business quarter is pleasantly situated overlooking the well-stocked, colourful **Boscawen Public Gardens**, the **Model Yacht Pond** and **Boating Lake** for children. But the main attraction here is the magnificent **Beach** of firm, clean sand which, at low tide, extends nearly three miles between Droskyn Point and Ligger Point. Perranporth is noted for its surf riding and the unequalled opportunities for indulging in this exhilarating pastime form one of its chief attractions. The district is wild and romantic and the pure Atlantic breezes exceptionally healthy and invigorating. The coast scenery is varied. To the north are the vast sandy towans rolling towards Holywell Bay: to the south, the towering, rugged cliffs of **Droskyn Point,** with their attractive rock archways, caves and pools. Not all these arches are natural formations, although the sea has modified their original shape. Some are disused mine workings, cut in the sixteenth and seventeenth centuries in the course of exploiting the Droskyn Lode of tin, copper, and silver-bearing lead ores. The hutments at the Point house a collection of scientific instruments for measuring the velocity of waves at sea-bed level.

At the foot of the hill on the north side of the town are camping and caravan parks well provided with amenities for a happy social life. Principal tennis courts are those of the Perranporth Lawn Tennis Club.

The **Golf Links** are about half a mile north-eastwards from the town, on the cliffs and sand-dunes overlooking the sea, affording a glorious view of the coast scenery between Newquay and St. Ives. There is a spacious club-house. Teas are generally available, but lunches must be booked beforehand with the stewardess.

At Trevellas, half-a-mile along the St. Agnes road, are the headquarters of the Cornish Gliding and Flying Club. Holiday members are welcomed, with instruction if desired.

Excursions from Perranporth

Perranporth is a good centre for enjoyable excursions by road to all parts of Western Cornwall, and particularly the interesting stretch of coast between the Gannel Estuary and St. Ives Bay. Motorists will have little difficulty in joining any of the routes given on pp. 147–158 or at the head of our descriptions of the various places usually visited.

To St. Piran's Lost Church (*see also p.* 48).

By Road.—Follow the Newquay road (passing the post office), climbing steeply past golf links. In just over 1 mile, where main road bends sharply to right, keep straight on (past some cottages on left) along a lane for half a mile until, facing the next turn on right, a white gate—The Gear Gate—is seen in the wall on left. Pass through gate (no fee is chargeable as the Trustees have a right of way to the church), and follow the track marked by white painted stones; short cuts are obvious here and there.

By the Sands (but observe the tide).—Follow the shore north-eastwards from Perranporth for about a mile. Where the steep cliffs give place to sandhills for a short distance strike inland. On reaching crest of slope, walk in direction of distant church spire (that of Cubert) and then follow the path descending to the right. This leads in a very short distance to the concrete building housing the remains of the oratory.

The two routes may well be combined to form a loop tour; but in setting out from the church for Gear Gate attention should be paid to the white stones indicating the path. Standing above the church and facing the cross, the gate lies well away to the *right*; the path continuing past the cross to the old cottage is that to Cubert (*see* p. 46).

The lane facing Gear Gate leads in half a mile to Rose and **St. Piran's Round** (*see* p. 57), and on to Goonhavern.

Legend declares that **St. Piran** floated over from Ireland on a millstone—a story possibly arising from the fact that he brought over an altar-stone (the ancient Irish altar stones were like miniature millstones in shape). He arrived in Cornwall about 500, and built a church close to

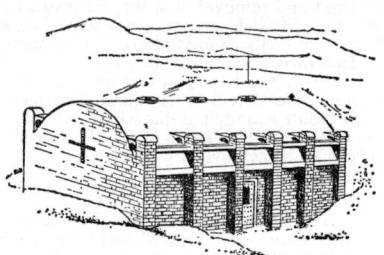

55

the spot where he landed. The present building is probably of the sixth or seventh century. Numerous stories are told of the life and miracles of St. Piran, who is the traditional patron saint of tinners. His feast is still kept on March 5. At the close of a long and successful ministry he died about 530 and is believed to have been buried beneath the altar of his oratory. In the course of time the sands drifted for miles over the land, completely burying the church, and the inhabitants were powerless to stop the invasion. Unable to rescue their lost church, the people built another, a few hundred yards east of the ruins, on the spot where now stands the Perran Cross alluded to below. This building remained, though frequently threatened with the same fate as its predecessor, until 1420, when it was considerably enlarged. The second church has been excavated and represents the plan of a typical Cornish church. The latter continued until 1804, when, further inundations of sand being imminent, it was removed to Perranzabuloe, 2 miles south-east of Perranporth.

The first excavation since the oratory was buried beneath the sand took place in 1835. Before this, observers had seen the tops of the walls protruding above the sand levels. It was found to be only a little building, some 30 feet in outside length. The inside length is only 25 feet. The width of the interior is 13 feet in the chancel and a foot less in the nave. It had a pitched roof with gables and one small window together with a stone seat running all round the interior. Traces were found of the shrine in which the relics of St. Piran were kept when not being carried about the county, from church to church, for popular veneration. With only one window it is assumed that the services must have been carried on by the light of tapers. The masonry is of the rudest kind, there being no attempt at regular courses. During excavations in 1835 several skeletons were found about two feet below the floors. Three of them had their feet lying underneath the altar and were without heads. The three heads lay between the knees of one of the skeletons. These remains were assumed to be those of martyrs who suffered for the faith St. Piran preached. Myriads of burials must have taken place around the ancient oratory. Gilbert—a Cornish historian who wrote at the beginning of the last century—speaks of whole rows of perfect skeletons being disclosed by the drifting sand.

After the excavations of 1835 the building suffered another inundation of sand and removal of stone, but steps were taken at length to protect it by enclosing it in a concrete outer cover, so that the ancient remains are safe from further molestation. For admission see p. 48.

The surrounding and interior sand has been cleared away, disclosing the doorway, window, stone benches, and floor, so that within the concrete shell it is possible to walk round the exterior of the ancient walls.

Sir John Arundell, in his will dated 1483, left 40s. to provide honourable protection for St. Piran's head. What has become of this relic is a mystery. There is some diversity of opinion as to the burial-place of the saint himself.

Perran Cross is one of the finest stones in the county, a great round-headed monolith 8 feet 10 inches in height. Documentary evidence has revealed that it has been standing on its present site for a thousand years.

NEWQUAY, PADSTOW, PORT ISAAC

English Miles

0   1   2   3   4

WARD, LOCK & CO. LIMITED, LONDON

© John Bartholomew & Son Ltd, Edinburgh

Roscarrock
Rumps
Newland
Pentire Pt.
Padstow Bay

Gulland Rock
Beacon
Pepper Hole
Butter Hole
Watch Ho.
Stepper Pt.

Gurley Rock
Gunver Hd.
Merope I.
Porthmissen Bridge
Lellissick
The Doom
Harbour Cove
Crugmeer
PADSTOW

TREVOSE Hd.
Lt. Ho. 243
L.B. Sta.
66
Dinas Hd.
Booby's Bay
Trevose
Polventon or Mother Ive's Bay
Harlyn Bay
Trevone B.
Porthmissen
Porthcothan
Trethillick
Pleasant Place
204
St Cadoc
Trevone
Treator
152
Constantine Bay
Harlyn
St Constantine Ch.
Treneague
Trelowsa
188
Sunny corner
Treyarnon Beach
Treyarnon
Towan
Inn.
St Merryn
Treggelles 195
Tregarden
86
Trevisker
Pepper Cove
Fox Cove
Trethias
Trehemborne
Shop
Tr. Trevorgus
Treravel
Carnivas
Trevoyan
Rosken
High Lanes
231
Tregonn
Lit.
Petherick
Porthcothan Beach
Trevorrick
Tregolds
Trebunick
Tregolds
Porthmear
Trevethan
Porthcothan
Aerodrome
Treleigh
Butter Coves
Penrire
Trevemedar
Treginegar
262
Tresert
Park Hd.
89
Penrose
184
Treburrick
St Ervan
250
Rumford
Trevibban
Diggory's I.
Tregona
Inn
Trerair
Queen Bess
Bedruthan Steps
Engollan
Trembleath
Trevengenon
338
Pendarves I.
Carnewas
Townhill
Trevisker
Pendarves Pt. (N.T.)
Carnewas I.
327
Camp
Eddystone
Trerathick Pt.
313
St Eval
415
Trenance Pt.
Bears Downs
492
Trenance Hotel
Trevilledor
Denzell Downs
Mawgan Porth
21
Moreland
Berryl's Pt. Co. Sta.
Gluvian
Denzell
Beacon Cove
Vale of Lanherne
Ford
Winnards
Rose
Livelow Hd.
Cas.
Lanvean
Trevarrian
Camp
310
Whitewater
Talskid
279
St Mawgan
Trefulrian Hotel
Watergate Bay
Tredggus
Trenowth
349
Drewan
St Co.
Bedrugga
Carnanton
Traskeval
Halvegor
Boswongey
Horse Rk.
173
Camp
Zacry's I.
226
Trebelzue
Trenoon
244
Trewinol
Trevelgue
Trevelgue Hd.
Tregaswith
Higher Trekenning
361
Towan Hd.
Newquay
Columb Porth
Tregenna
257
Trebarva
Trevithick
333
Trekenning Ho.
174
Headland Hotel
Gazzle Bay
Atlantic Hotel
Inn
Porth Veor
St Columb Minor
St Eval's Well
Tregoose
Trebudannon
243
Fistral Bay
Trethellan
Victoria Hotel
Tretherras
Rialton
Penhall
Camp
Tehidy Hill
Yankelly
NEWQUAY
Trencreek
Trewollack
Penhall
Colan
281
Bosoughan
Killaworgey
Penpol
Trenance
Chapel
Bejowan
Pollawyn
299
Black Cross

St. Piran's Round. Take the main Newquay road from Perranporth (which runs north-west from the post office) and ascend the hill past the golf links. Keep to the main road round the sharp bend to the right and in 1¾ miles the signboard for Rose is reached. Continue past this until a grass space is reached on left, alongside a timber bungalow. St. Piran's Round can be seen from this point, on the left, about 30 yards to the north. **St. Piran's Round** is an ancient amphitheatre. The diameter is 130 feet, and the sloping bank, now covered with gorse and brambles, was once divided into seven tiers. The Round is one of the most perfect of its kind and is capable of accommodating 2,000 persons. Here the ancient Cornish miracle plays were performed. The Cornish Gorsedd was revived here in 1946, when large numbers of people attended the ceremony. The Round is scheduled as an Ancient Monument.

Trevaunance Cove, St. Agnes, a fine walk southward along the cliffs for about 4½ miles (*see* p. 62).

The road should be followed as it climbs steeply up the southern side of the valley, as far as a lane on the right just beyond the old explosives factory. This lane eventually reaches the coast near an abandoned mine at a scene of wild desolation. **Cligga Head, 2** miles from Perranporth, is a fine bluff cliff. Ahead, in the distance, rises St. Agnes Beacon, a land-mark for many miles around. It is difficult going most of the way to the steep descent to the Trevellas Valley, opening to **Trevellas Porth** with a stream flowing on to the beach. In spite of abandoned mines and heaps of tailings, it is curiously picturesque. An equally steep climb out of the valley leads over the hill to the beautiful **Trevaunance Cove, St. Agnes** (*see* p. 62), 4½ miles from Perranporth by the cliffs. At low tide a short scramble over rocks saves the climb over the hill (where is the fenced track of the famous *Bluehills*, climax of the annual Motor Cycle Reliability Trials) p. 61.

Cubert, 3½ miles, thence to either the Holy Well (2 miles) or Crantock (1¾ miles), farther (p. 46). Follow the route to **Gear Gate** given in the first excursion, but instead of turning through gate keep along lane until it makes a sharp turn to right, when a path will be seen on left crossing the marshland to Trebisken farm, as described on p. 48. After heavy rains avoid this path and continue by the lane which branches left past Trebellan. Cubert church is prominent ahead. For route thence to **Crantock** (*see* p. 39). Continue to Newquay and return by bus.

Perranzabuloe, 1¾ miles south-east of Perranporth, is the "Churchtown." A marble tablet records the fact that "The first stone of the parish church was laid in the year 1804, after two former ones had been overwhelmed with the sand of the desert in which they were imprudently built." The old church—the second of the St. Piran churches—was erected in 1178, but its tower and some small parts were subsequently removed to Lambourne. The walls are more or less intact beneath the sand. This church received thorough restoration in 1879. The old font from the second church has been preserved, and the old bench-ends were utilized for the pulpit.

St. Piran's Well was situated about half a mile eastward of the church at Perranzabuloe. Its spring having been destroyed, the scattered stones of the building were reconstructed in the grounds of Chiverton.

Caer Kief and **Caer Dane Castles** are close by. Whitaker says the latter should be Caer Don, not being a Danish camp at all. At Ventongimps, in the neighbourhood, an urn was discovered, nearly 5 feet in height, its general appearance indicating Roman origin. Numerous barrows dot the country for miles around.

FOR PLACES WESTWARD

OF THE AREA COVERED BY THIS GUIDE

SEE THE RED GUIDE TO

WEST CORNWALL

Includes St. Ives, Carbis Bay, Penzance, Newlyn, The Lizard, Land's End and the Scilly Isles.

Perranporth to St. Ives

These twenty odd miles of high rocky coastline contain much wild and lovely cliff and moorland scenery with occasional descents to the delightful sandy beaches at Trevaunance Cove, St. Agnes; Chapel Porth; Porthtowan and Portreath. The larger towns lie some four to five miles inland.

Walkers who set out to follow this rugged, indented coast will find ample reward in the magnificent views both seawards and inland. There is also much to interest the geologist and the naturalist. It is, however, rather hard going most of the way owing to the ascents and descents encountered where steep valleys cut across the route and ample time should be allowed for this when making plans.

Motorists see little of the actual coast until **Trevaunance Cove, St. Agnes** is reached. At that point, and onwards, the extensive and beautiful views from St. Agnes Beacon Drive, and again during the descents to Porthtowan and Portreath, also from the coast road to Hayle, will surely delight the most difficult to please.

On arriving at Peterville, St. Agnes, where five roads meet, motorists should bear right for Trevaunance Cove until the Car Park is reached in a little under half a mile. To continue to **Porthtowan** by road, *via* Beacon Drive, return to Peterville, cross main road and turn up British Road, right into Vicarage Road and Churchtown for Trevaunance Road (one-way traffic operating). Continue right round Beacon Drive for about two miles and past the turning for Chapel Porth. Take next turning to right at cross-roads which, in about a mile, passes through the pretty hamlet of **Mingoose**. Take the ascent beyond with caution as road narrows and becomes steeper. On reaching main road at top, opposite *Victory Inn*, bear right and in half a mile a grand view of the sea, beach and cliffs at Porthtowan is obtained. The descent should be made with caution. Continuing on from Porthtowan turn left half-way up the hill. In 1½ miles, at the third turning to right by the second signboard, bear off right along a narrow road with castellated stone walls on either side, which skirts the hamlet of Cambrose, and, after passing over a pretty stream, joins the main road from Redruth to Portreath (B3300), at which bear right. **Portreath** is reached in about 1¾ miles along the well-wooded valley road.

Three miles south of Perranporth as the crow flies, or 4½ by road (B3285), brings the visitor to—

St. Agnes and Trevaunance Cove

Access.—Paddington to Truro, thence by bus. The former branchline is now closed.

Bank.—*Lloyds* Mon., Tues. and Fri. 10 a.m.–12.30 p.m., 1.30–3 p.m. Also Thursday in July–August.

Bathing.—Very good, from firm, clean sand. Surf-riding popular.

Boating.—Motor and rowing boats can be hired from the beach for short trips or sea fishing.

Bus Services.—To Truro, Redruth, Trevellas, Perranporth, etc. Time-tables are exhibited at key points.

Car Park.—Adjoining beach at Cove and at Vicarage Road.

Distances by Road.—Truro, 8 miles; Redruth, 7; Newquay, 12; Falmouth, 15; St. Ives, 19; Boscastle, 49; Penzance, 25; Land's End, 35.

Early Closing Day.—Wednesday.

Entertainments.—St. Agnes Horticultural and Handicrafts Show. Regatta and Gala in August. Annual Floral Dance. Cinema, *Regal*, Vicarage Road.

Golf.—At Perranporth, *see* p. 54.

Hotels.—*Driftwood Spars*, Trevaunance Cove; *The Pentlands; Wynberg*, Goonown; *Peterville Inn; Railway; Rosevean*, Rosemundy.

Hunting.—Four Burrow Pack, Scorrier.

Licensing Hours.—10.30–2.30 and 5.30–10.30. (Summer 11). Sundays, 12–2, 7–10.30.

Places of Worship.—*St. Agnes* (Parish Church). The *Methodist Church*, British Road.

Post Office.—Churchtown, 9 a.m.–1 p.m., 2–5.30 p.m., Wednesdays 9 a.m.–1 p.m. only.

Population.—Approx. 4,200.

At one time, St. Agnes was a busy and thriving tin-mining centre. Tin then being mined in the district was generally acknowledged to be the best in Cornwall. As this once important industry declined so, perhaps, fortunately for the residents, occasional visitors chanced to discover this small and ancient Cornish town and very quickly learned to appreciate its quiet dignity and unusually beautiful surroundings.

There has probably been less written in praise of St. Agnes, its Beacon and Trevaunance Cove than of any other beauty spot in the kingdom but, of those who have once seen it for themselves, few have been able to resist its many unique charms and many return regularly year after year.

To those who delight in glorious seascapes, high, open moorland plentifully dappled with sea-pinks, gorse and heather, with intersecting valleys and streams leading down to the sea, St. Agnes has much to offer. It is a healthy little town. The air is superb, the blend of pure, bracing Atlantic breezes with soft moorland air having a rare tonic effect on the whole system.

Probably the greatest charm of St. Agnes lies in the infinite variety and beauty of its immediate surroundings. The town is built high up on the slopes of a hill and the scene changes every few yards as new and delightful vistas open up.

The Parish Church of St. Agnes was rebuilt over 100 years ago. Unlike most Cornish churches, it boasts both a tower and a spire. The handsome lych-gate was added in 1935 to the memory of John Coulter Hancock. Baptisms are recorded from 1653 and marriages and burials from 1674. The famous artist John Opie was born at Harmony Cot, St. Agnes, in 1761. He died in 1807 and is buried in the crypt of St. Paul's Cathedral. The cottage where he was born is still to be seen by Trevellas Downs.

St. Agnes is bigger than appears at first sight. It meanders in all directions and the parish embraces **Chapel Porth** and **Porthtowan** on the south-west and **Blue Hills Mine** (where the famous Easter Saturday Hill Climb is held), **Trevellas, Trevellas Porth** and most of **Trevellas Airfield** (famous Fighter Station in World War II and now a popular Gliding venue) on the north-east; to the south—**Mount Hawke** and **Blackwater;** and to the east, the hamlet of **Mithian** (*Miner's Arms*). The whole district abounds in beautiful and health-giving walks and rambles.

The hub of the town centres on the parish church and is known as Churchtown. Where the five roads meet at foot of Town-hill is Peterville. Goonlaze runs from Peterville along the Trevellas road and, a few hundred yards beyond, Wheal Kitty is reached by the first turn to the left. The cluster of cottages and bungalows at Trevaunance Cove is referred to locally as "The Quay" from the fact that there was once a small harbour at the cove. The hill descending opposite the Railway Hotel is Rosemundy, while up the hill to the right is Goonown. A few hundred yards farther on, past the Recreation Ground, is Goonbell. Proceeding inland along Vicarage Road (continuation of Churchtown) the first turning to the right leads to Goonvrea. At the cross-roads farther on, that to the left leads to Mingoose, that to the right to Higher Ball (which bisects Beacon Drive) while Chapel Porth is straight on.

"Stippy Stappy," the first narrow lane on left a few yards down Town-hill, is a short cut to Trevaunance Cove for those on foot. The stone cottages, on the left going down, drop below each other so steeply that some distance away they seem to resemble giant steps—hence the name. Behind them rises a well-wooded hillside, the haunt of owls, woodpeckers and other local bird life. In the spring the turf under the trees bordering the lane is brilliant with masses of bluebells. A pleasant stream accompanies the path for the last hundred yards where it joins Quay Road, leading down the valley to the sea, some five minutes' walk away. Another way down to Quay is by Trevaunance Road and Friendly Retreat where there are seats and a good view over the Cove. Farther is a steep path towards the Quay. When the road is reached it may be crossed and a path taken between trees and over the heather to the cliffs whence by turning right a return may be made to the Quay.

Trevaunance Cove

Passing a cluster of cottages and a few bungalows on either side; the stores, and parking ground on the left and finally the café on the right, the visitor arrives at Trevaunance Cove —without doubt one of the most lovely natural rocky inlets to be found anywhere round the coast.

On a sunny morning, with a few clouds, the colour of the sea here is truly magnificent and worth travelling a very long way to enjoy. Almost every conceivable shade of blue, green and purple mingle to delight the eye and thrill the heart. The effect of vivid colouring is further enhanced by the rich buffs and browns of the great rocky headlands which rise steeply from the sea on either side.

Below high-water mark the beach is of firm, clean sand. Bathing, particularly surf riding, is excellent. But, as with all rocky coasts, it is definitely dangerous to swim out to sea, especially at low water or on an ebb tide. A few chalets at the foot of the towering cliffs may be rented on a weekly basis and deck chairs may be hired. A shelter, with seats, is close at hand in the event of a shower, with toilets adjoining.

St. Agnes Beacon

The town is flanked on the south-west by St. Agnes Beacon (630 ft., National Trust), a prominent land and sea mark for many miles around. The ascent is quite easy at one or two points and will well repay the effort for the unique and extensive views in all directions. On a clear day it is possible to pick out over 30 church towers from the summit; to look across south-eastwards into Falmouth Harbour and south-westwards to St. Michael's Mount. Inland, the "Cornish Giants," Brown Willy (1,375 ft.) and Rough Tor (1,312 ft.), approximately 40 miles distant as the crow flies, can be seen under favourable conditions.

A good motor road, **Beacon Drive,** some two miles in length, encircles the base. **St. Agnes Head** may be seen from the seaward side of Beacon Drive. A mile offshore, although appearing much nearer, and a few points to the north, are the **Bawden Rocks** or **Man and His Man.** As the road itself is some hundreds of feet above sea-level, grand panoramic views are obtained along the coast ranging in the south-west to St. Ives and beyond, to Trevose Head with its Lighthouse in the north-east, while inland the "white pyramids" of the China Clay burrows in the St. Austell area are prominent features. From the seaward side of Beacon Drive, a mile out from Churchtown, a grand view may be had of the remarkable Coloured Cliffs on the Trevellas (or north-east) side of Trevaunance Cove. The brilliant colours are mainly due to the presence of various minerals in the rock and range from pink and red to pale blue—a unique and very beautiful sight.

Chapel Porth,

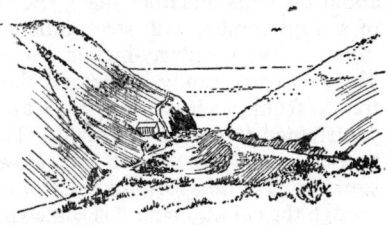

a miniature rocky cove about 2 miles south-westward, is a favourite walk over the cliffs from St. Agnes, or may be reached by car in a little over a mile from the Goonvrea side of Beacon Drive. The road is steep in parts, narrow and rough and ends at the car park and café adjoining the beach. At low tide there is an excellent sandy beach and there are many fine caves. It is National Trust property and an ideal spot for a quiet rest.

Porthtowan,

(1 mile beyond Chapel Porth over the cliffs or 3 miles from St. Agnes by road) is a delightful, natural playground with extensive sands flanked by noble headlands. Porthtowan is a rising little place, at present in process of development. Though the foreshore is excellent for beach sports requiring plenty of room, it is unfortunate that bathing can be very dangerous. There are a few small shops, post office, cafés and parking places.

Portreath

Bathing.—Very good, though caution is necessary on an ebb tide or at low water. Surf riding is popular though warning notices should be observed. Surf boards may be hired.
Bus to Redruth and Camborne.
Car Park.—Adjoining and overlooking beach.

Distances.—St. Agnes, 7 miles; Redruth, 4; Hayle, 8; St. Ives, 13.
Golf.—Tehidy Park Golf Course, 1 mile.
Hotel.—*Portreath*, The Square.
Railway.—Nearest station Redruth, Western Region line, 4 miles.
Church.—St. Mary's, dedicated in 1963. Sundays at 10 a.m. and 6 p.m.

To obtain one's first sight of Portreath from the Hayle coast road, as it winds steeply down to the car park, is to see it at its best. The rich blue sea, the sandy beach, the lofty cliffs, and the quaint old harbour combine to provide a beautiful and typically Cornish picture. Nowadays this port is little used, but until fairly recently small coasting colliers edged their way through the narrow harbour entrance to discharge coal for the surrounding district.

Portreath, once known as Basset's Cove, is picturesque in a Continental way, with terraced houses and bungalows dotted about the cliffs on either side. The village is set along the base of a deep combe, with steep hills on either hand, and a long (now disused) railway-incline ascending from the harbour. There is a fine sandy beach and the easy accessibility of Portreath from such centres as Camborne and Redruth has contributed to its recent growth. There is an hotel and guesthouses, and houses and bungalows can be rented during summer. The hills forming the Combe are delightfully wooded, though the country round is somewhat bare. At half-tide a fine cave, with a bathing-pool in the centre, can be visited, under the cliffs to the west of the combe. The big rock which stands up so boldly at sea is the **Gull Rock.** The peaceful view seaward from Portreath during summer gives little idea of the great seas experienced during winter storms. The entrance to the harbour is narrow and almost impossible to approach in rough weather. The new St. Mary's Church was dedicated in 1963.

The road to Redruth (4 miles) is interesting for the first mile, as it lies up the beautiful Portreath valley. At the fork in a mile and a half the telegraph wires go to the right (the shortest way, but over a steep hill), while the signpost points to the left for Redruth. The latter road is level but uninteresting. Some water-wheels, etc., are at work, supplying the motive power to stamps for obtaining tin and arsenic.

Port Isaac

Rock, near Padstow

Trevone Bay

Perranporth

Illogan stands on a hill between Portreath and Redruth.

It was the birthplace of the famous *Tangye Brothers* who founded the great engineering firm which still bears their name at Cornwall Works, Birmingham. The house where the family lived is quite close to the church.

The church, which was entirely re-erected in 1848, contains the tombs of the Bassets, and a fine window in memory of the late head of that family. In the churchyard is an ancient granite cross, 5 feet high. The fourteenth-century tower of the old church stands detached. The font is of the same period. The register of baptisms dates from 1539; marriages from 1600, and burials from 1540.

At Pool, near Illogan Highway, the great engineer *Richard Trevithick* was born in 1771. Amongst his other achievements he was the inventor of the High-Pressure Steam Engine and of the first Steam Road Carriage to be used in England—which made its appearance in Camborne on Christmas Eve 1801. The large Cornwall Technical College at Pool has over 5,000 students.

Tehidy, formerly in the possession of the Basset family, was purchased by public subscription after the 1914–18 war and converted for use as a hospital to form the Cornwall County War Memorial.

The attractive Tehidy Park Golf Course is open to visitors.

PORTREATH TO GWITHIAN

A good road runs close to the cliffs for a great part of the way and affords some fine views of this wild coast. The walk along the cliffs is about six and a half miles. Motorists cross the stream by the bridge alongside car park, ascend the hill to the left and bear to the right at the top. Walkers, after crossing the stream by the bridge beside car park ascend the hill to the right on to the North Coast footpath, which passes a guest-house on the edge of the cliff. Then they continue down behind a little cove and up the broad green path by the tele-graph wires until they go to the right, when the cliffs are soon reached. This is a favourite walk from Portreath, as the cliff scenery is very fine. The path is sometimes close to the edge of the cliff, and sometimes a little inland (to cross a small headland or avoid a landslip), for all this coast is crumbling. Combes are best crossed as near their heads as possible, and they should be carefully reconnoitred for paths, as most are a tangle of brambles. Passing **Ralph's Cupboard,** a curiously shaped inlet in the rock, **Samphire Island** and **Crane Islands** come in view. On the mainland, opposite Crane Islands, is to be seen an early cliff castle. The downs are wild near the sea, but half a mile inland are some plantations. In the distance occasional glimpses of Godrevy Lighthouse on the island off Godrevy Point are obtained. Passing **Deadman's Cove** and **Hell's Mouth** keep to the cliff path and round **Navax Point,** and so to Godrevy Island and over the Towans and the Red River to Gwithian. About half a mile from Navax Point is the **Seal Cave,** which can be reached by boat. Much of the land around Godrevy is National Trust property.

On nearing—

Gwithian

(*Hotel;* buses to Hayle, etc.) there is a magnificent view of beautiful St. Ives Bay. Where there is a long break in the cliffs, near the point at which the stream known as the Red River flows into the sea, it is a scene of sandy desolation and even the trees sheltering the village have been so bent by successive storms as to wear the appearance of breaking waves, through which the roofs of the houses and the church tower project like rocks.

Gwithian Church is dedicated to SS. Felix and Gothian, and was rebuilt in 1866, only part of the chancel wall and the tower of the old building remaining. The font bowl is Norman, and has been renovated. The lych-gate was constructed from materials taken from the south arcade, and in the churchyard is an ancient round-headed cross.

There is little to detain tourists at Gwithian, and the chances are they will look in vain for the remains of **St. Gwithian's Oratory.** These are near the Red River near the bridge on road coming down from the cliffs to the north, but mound and wall are not easily identified. The oratory was buried for many hundred years in the sands. Possibly erected in the ninth century, it was, like that of St. Piran, laid bare about a century ago by a shifting of the sand. Internally it was about 45 feet long by 15 feet wide. St. Gwithian is the proto-martyr of Cornwall. In this parish are **Trevarnon Rounds,** old earthworks probably used in the Civil War.

The shore hereabouts is fringed by dunes and cliffs and there is a fine two-mile walk along the sands. Between the Red River and the Hayle estuary are numerous chalet and caravan camps as well as permanent bungalows.

Camborne

Although in no sense one of Cornwall's holiday resorts, Camborne is an interesting place and one of the few big industrial centres near the north coast of the Duchy. It is a busy and pleasant town in spite of the proximity of several important and well-known engineering and other industrial undertakings. At **Tuckingmill,** just before entering Camborne from Redruth, will be seen a tablet let into the wall of the big works on left, which records the fact that William Bickford of Camborne was the inventor of the *Safety Fuse,* which has since saved countless lives of miners all over the world. Arthur Woolf, a Camborne engineer, is generally credited with having been the first to adapt the early steam engines for use in connection with mining.

His more famous colleague, Richard Trevithick, who invented the high-pressure steam engine (*see* p. 65), was born close by, at Pool. There is a fine statue of Trevithick fronting the Passmore Edwards Library. One of the more important buildings is the School of Mines where those making mining their career receive valuable instruction. Owing to the decline in the mining industry in Cornwall most graduates take up positions overseas. Apart from its busy industries Camborne is the shopping centre for the scattered rural districts of which it is the hub. There is an extensive public park and the main public buildings include the Museum, Market, Municipal Offices, Masonic Hall and the County School for girls.

There are many good walks in the district, such as to the pretty village of Treslothan, or Pendarves, while Portreath on the north coast is only 4 miles distant.

Redruth

Buses.—To Newquay; to Illogan and Portreath; to St. Day and Carharrack; to Penryn and Falmouth; to Scorrier, Chacewater and Truro; to St. Agnes and Perranporth; to Helston and Land's End.

Car Parks.—Fair Meadow, near Station, *fee.*; Green Lane, *fee.*; Penryn Street, Clinton Road and Pednandrea have free parking places on the highway. New Cut, free.

Cinemas.—*Regal*, Fore Street.

Early Closing Day.—Thursday.

Hotels.—*Druids*, Penryn Street; *London; Red Lion.*

Licensing Hours.—10.30–2.30 and 5.30–10.30; Sundays, 12–2, 7–10.30.

Market Day.—Friday.

Population.—Camborne — Redruth — 38,300.

Post Office.— Fore Street.

Road Route from Newquay *via* Trenance Valley, Trevemper Bridge, Zelah, and the Land's End road.

Railway Station on Western Region line in centre of town.

Redruth clings to the sides of two steep hills, a crowded, somewhat old-fashioned town with modern additions and amenities. (For those in a hurry to complete their journey a by-pass runs from Mount Ambrose to the western end of the town, and is clearly indicated.) Redruth is an important commercial shopping town and an excellent touring centre. Yet visitors might be interested to run in on a Friday to see what a busy Cornish town is like on market day. Redruth was the old mining capital of Cornwall with an important Exchange, but Camborne with its School of Mines has now superseded it.

Every other house seems as if it could tell a tale. From the balcony of Bank House John Wesley preached, and at **Gwennap Pit** (only a mile or so out of the town on the St. Day road, then sharp right at the entry to St. Day) he exhorted tens of thousands (30,000 was his estimate, "and I shall scarce see a larger

congregation till we meet in the air," was his comment). A glance at some of the capacious dissenting chapels in Redruth will help one to realise the hold Wesley had on Cornishmen. Every Whit-Monday the Methodists hold a mass service at Gwennap Pit.

George Fox, founder of the Society of Friends,

was in 1655 imprisoned in the King's Head Tavern, a fifteenth-century house now demolished. Not many people know that gas-lighting was invented in Redruth, in 1792, by William Murdock, a Scottish engineer. The cottage and shop in Cross Street, in which he made the experiments which led to the great discovery, is still to be seen. On the wall facing the narrow lane at the side is a tablet which reads:

"William Murdock lived in this house, 1782–98. Made the first locomotive here, and tested it in 1784. Invented gas-lighting, and used it in this house in 1792."

South Crofty is the only tin-mine still working in the Camborne–Redruth area. The Company possesses leases covering an area over two miles long and a mile wide. Included in this area is the Old Dolcoath Mine, which worked to a depth of 3,000 feet. Now disused, it was at one time the deepest in the world. Passmore Edwards, the journalist and newspaper proprietor, who gave many free libraries to Cornwall, was born at Blackwater, north-east of Redruth.

Chacewater is a small but pretty village on the Redruth–Truro road. James Watt, the celebrated engineer, is said to have lived here for a time while working on the first Steam Pumping Engine to be used in Cornish mines.

On the left of the road when leaving Redruth in the direction of Camborne, the wild, rugged hill known as—

Carn Brea

rises abruptly in the centre of a lonely district. This hill is chiefly granite, wild and imposing in its rugged outline. It was probably a military station in Neolithic times. The hill is 750 feet above sea-level, and affords magnificent views on each side of the county. Here are the restored remains of an ancient castle, occupied, according to William of Worcester (1478), by Sir John Basset, whose family were the principal landowners in the neighbourhood. Some huge rocks will be found on Carn Brea, and one or two roomy caves. Of interest to archæologists are the foundations of many hut circles. Here was the centre of a large settlement. In June, 1749, a number of pure gold coins were found which, being sold by weight, realised sixteen pounds sterling. A cooking hearth and stone weapons found here are to be seen in the Museum at Truro.

The conspicuous granite monument, 90 feet high, was erected by public subscription to Francis Lord de Dunstanville and Basset. At one time a spiral staircase ascended to the top. On a clear day the sea on either side of the county is plainly seen, and away to the south-west the rocky, castle-crowned islet of St. Michael's Mount rises from Mount's Bay.

Between Redruth and Gwennap is the hill of *Carn Marth*, the view from which rivals that from Carn Brea.

Padstow and Wadebridge

PADSTOW

Approach.—Connecting bus services from Bodmin Road, on Western Region main line. Road route, see pp. 6–9.

Banks.—*Barclays, Lloyds, Midland,* near Quay.

Bathing Beaches.—Down river at Chapel Bar; at Ship-my-Pumps; below Chapel Stile (town beach); St. George's Cove and Harbour Cove (Tregirls Beach). It is essential to pay heed to warning notices when posted at the various beaches.

Buses.—Buses connect Padstow with St. Columb and Newquay, and with various outlying villages and porths.

Car Park.—Parks on North and South Quays and the Lawn.

Distances.—London, 246; Plymouth, 44; Wadebridge, 8; Bodmin, 15; St. Columb, 9; Tintagel, 21; Stepper Point (by cliff path), 2½; St. Merryn, 2½; Trevose Lighthouse, 5; Harlyn Bay, 2½; Newquay, 15.

Excursions.—Coach and bus tours to all parts of Cornwall.

Ferry (no cars) across the Camel estuary to Rock (for the golf links), runs from North Quay unless the water is low, when it starts from the beach. Running hours vary with the season and light, roughly 8 a.m. to 8 p.m. summer; 8 a.m. to 7 p.m., spring and autumn; 8 a.m. to 5 p.m. winter.

Fishing.—Fairly good fishing for bass, etc., from boats. Fine area for mackerel.

Licences to fish for salmon and trout in the Camel and some other rivers obtainable from Radford's (Padstow) Ltd., Duke Street.

Golf.—Across the estuary at Rock (St. Enodoc) and at Trevose (see p. 75).

Hotels.—*Metropole; Dinas; Old Ship; North Quay,* North Quay; *Cross House* (private), Cross Street.

Licensing Hours.—11–2.30 and 5.30–10, Sundays, 12–2, 7–10.

Life-boat.—Padstow life-boat is now stationed at Trevose.

Places of Worship, with hours of Sunday services: *St. Petroc's* (Parish Church)—8, 11, and 6; *Methodist*—11 and 6; *Roman Catholic*—1st, 3rd and 5th at 11, 2nd and 4th at 9.30.

Population.—2,560 (inc. Trevone).

Post and Telegraph Office.—Close to Harbour quay, 8.30 a.m. to 6 p.m.; Sundays and Bank Holidays, 9 a.m. to 10.30 a.m.

Road Routes from Newquay (16 miles) *via* St. Columb Minor and Major (where turn left on entering). Keep to left at Winnards Perch, about 2 miles farther. Padstow is entered by a steep descent with awkward turns at foot.

Another route is *via* Bedruthan Steps (*see* p. 45), whence follow the narrow road *via* Porthcothan and St. Merryn.

Tennis at Lawn Recreation Ground, where are Car Park and Children's playground.

Scattered down the slopes and at the foot of a steep cliff is the ancient port of Padstow (formerly Petrockstow). Once a corporate borough governed by a mayor and burgesses, with a charter granted in 1583 by Queen Elizabeth, it seems now to have awakened from a long sleep, for no one knows when the mayoral functions were last performed.

It is a place of great antiquity. In the ancient Cornu-British tongue it was called *Lodenek,* whilst in 1291, in the records of a

pastoral visitation, the name is given as "*Aldestowe*". In former days it was a ship-building port of some importance, but steam and, later, motor vessels gradually replaced the old Padstow schooners. The trade of the port was at one time largely with Canada for timber; later fishing, chiefly for soles, became the principal business. Now it is mainly a residential country town and shopping centre for a wide area. The railway authorities improved the dock accommodation at great expense some years ago. It is unfortunate that the sand bar across the estuary prevents large vessels entering the harbour but as many as 25 trawlers come in on a wild day. Boats bearing the distinctive letters PW (meaning they are registered at Padstow) will be found in almost every harbour along this coast.

The quaint, busy little place, so delightfully situated, is now realising that it possesses every necessary qualification of a holiday resort, with none of the drawbacks of the ordinary fishing village posing as such. First-class sailing and boating may be enjoyed, the chief drawbacks being swift tides and erratic breezes, greater hindrances to the novice than to the experienced. Owing to the position of Padstow on a peninsula, a great many different coves and bays can be easily visited. In the season daily coach excursions are run to all parts and there are daily cruises round the several headlands and small islands off the coast.

The town has a fair sprinkling of shops, an *Institute* with billiards, recreation and reading-rooms, and a branch of the County Library in Market Place. There are also a cinema and a Masonic Hall. From the summit of **Dennis Hill** fine views are obtained not only across and up the estuary, but also out to sea. The 56-foot monument commemorates the Jubilee of Queen Victoria.

St. Petroc's Church

is of great interest and has been extensively restored. St. Petroc, according to Fuller, was a Welshman who, after being educated in Ireland, came to Padstow in A.D. 518. On the wall of the chancel is a small sculptured effigy, usually said to represent St. Petroc. The stained-glass windows are fine. The fifteenth-century font has sculptured figures of the twelve apostles. The thirteenth-century tower of flat slaty rock is much older than the rest of the church, which was enlarged and rebuilt in the fifteenth century. The flamboyant tracery of some of the windows in the south side of the chancel does not necessarily indicate a different period, but is more likely due to Continental influence. In the south aisle is a fifteenth-century carved sedilia made of four of the old bench-ends, two of which are in excellent preservation. The pulpit is sixteenth-century or possibly pre-Reformation and finely preserved. The rood-stairs will be noticed and some old bosses of the roof; also the angels on the wall plates in the south chapel, restored as a thank-offering for Peace.

There are numerous memorials, a striking one (at west end of south aisle) being to members of the Prideaux family. The ancient stocks are in the south porch. In the churchyard are three old crosses, one over the Prideaux family vault in front of the tower, found in the grounds of Prideaux Place and erected to the memory of three members of the family; another stands a little to the right of the south porch. Close to the gate in the south-east corner of the churchyard is the massive shaft of a cross supposed to be still older.

Padstow possesses many quaint corners, narrow and crooked by-ways and picturesque buildings. In Fentonluna Lane (*Monastery Well*), leading to Prideaux Place, is a renovated **Well,** now marked by a pump bearing the date 1592 on a modern stone at the top, with older lettering round the sides, on which "Prideau" and "Nicholas" may be read. Parallel to Fentonluna is the so-called High Street, an amazing little narrow lane tumbling down towards the Quay. On the North quay is an ancient building known as **Abbey House,** from which a subterranean passage was built to connect it with the monastery (destroyed by the Danes in 981) which formerly occupied the upper part of the town, including Prideaux Place. It is believed to have been the old Guild House of the Padstow merchants and dates from the fifteenth century. It contains some odd bits of stone tracery. **Raleigh's Court House,** on the South quayside, dates back to the sixteenth century. Here Raleigh held his Court and collected his legal dues as Warden of Cornwall.

At the top of the hill stands the imposing **Prideaux Place**, once known in olden days as Gwarthandrea. (*Not open to the public.*) It is the seat of J. C. F. Prideaux-Brune, Lord of the Manor, and was completed in 1585, though there have been some later additions. St. Petroc founded a monastery here, but this was destroyed by the Danes in 981. Prideaux Place crowns the hill and may be seen at a great distance. The castellated façade is of great length and very beautiful. Close by, an arch spans a side road and lends an air of antiquity to the scene. An ancient cross stands in the grounds.

The Hobby Horse

A quaint custom at Padstow are the "hobby-horse" dances on May Day. The Padstow May song, we fear, has been somewhat garbled. There are really two songs, "The Night Song" and the "Day Song". The former begins:

> "Unite and unite, and let us unite,
>   For summer is acome in today,
>   And whither we are going we all will unite,
>   In the merry month of May."

In the latter two choruses, to be repeated alternately, run:

> "And for to fetch the summer home, the summer and the May O,
>   For summer is acome O, and winter is ago."

and

> "With Hal-an-tow, and jolly rumble O,
>   For summer is acome O, and winter is ago,
>   And in every land O, the land that e'er we go."

The hobby-horse is a fearsome creature, with its ferocious mask, and more like a heathen god than a horse. Before the horse dances a man carrying a club called the "Teaser". The whole thing is grotesque, but is one of the most genuine folk customs surviving in England. In Cross Street will be noticed a cross let into the pavement. In the centre of this a maypole used to be set up as part of the "hobby-horse" celebrations. Now the maypole is set up in the Market Square.

"The hobby-horse is formed by a man encased in a cloth mask that conceals him. It is a formidable-looking creature, solemnly black, except for the vari-coloured stripes on cap and mask, with tall cap, flowing plume and tail, savage-looking oaken snappers, and a ferocious face mask. On the cap, one on each side of the upright stripes, are the letters O.B., which are carefully repeated on every new mask. The cap plume, tail, and decoration of the snappers are all of real horsehair. The snapper jaws are studded inside to increase the noise. They are worked by a string held by the man inside."

73

The dance is a rite of great antiquity. The death of the horse clearly represents the end of winter and the sudden upsurge of the dance, the new life which comes with the arrival of spring.

The Camel Estuary

Were it not for the sand bar at the mouth this natural harbour would be of greater use to mariners. The estuary, winding between grassy cliffs on one side and the lower sandy dunes on the other, is always beautiful, but especially so at high water. It averages about three-quarters of a mile in width, and is over 6 miles long. The entrance is guarded by **Pentire Point** (Rock side) and **Stepper Point** (Padstow side). The latter, 227 feet high, is surmounted by a small tower, or "day-mark", for shipping. It is a pretty walk of two and a half miles from Padstow by the path down the estuary to the Day-mark; starting from the harbour or turning to the right at the fork of the main street up the town, the two paths converging at the War Memorial Cross overlooking the estuary. A short distance before this a path turns down to the cove on the shore, which is the low-tide starting-place of the **Rock Ferry.** Continuing, the way soon drops down to the rocky inlet of **St. George's Well,** a perennially flowing spring in the rocks. Crossing the little stream, the path climbs steeply to **Gun Point,** whence it continues to **Harbour Cove,** locally known as Tregirls Beach, with fine sands, affording a fine view of the **Doom Bar.** When a heavy squall strikes the mouth of the harbour, whipping the water into foam from side to side, the significance of the name will be recognized. The Doom Bar, according to ancient legend, was the work of a mermaid. This mermaid was the protectress of the town, and when a young man mortally wounded her with an arrow she threw a handful of sand towards the town with a curse, and so the bar was formed. Month by month thousands of tons of sand are taken from the estuary for agricultural purposes, as it is rich in carbonate of lime. This has provided a considerable export activity for many years.

From the head of Harbour Cove the path can be followed along the coast past **Hawker's Cove** to Stepper Point, whence the walk may be continued round the coast to **Gunver Head,** or a return made to Padstow by striking up the path which follows the cliffs by Lelizzick Farm. Now on to Crugmeer and then by the old church path direct to Padstow or by road to Trethillick and Padstow.

A word must be said respecting the fine cliff scenery of the neighbourhood. The **Tregudda Gorge** is a grand sight at any time, and magnificent when the sea is rough. The gorge lies between three very fine sea stacks and the mainland. With a rare disregard for mere utilitarian interests the Lord of the Manor refuses to allow quarrying at this point.

Farther south is **Porthmissen Bridge,** a natural arch. Beyond the curious **Round Hole,** a blow hole, the coast bends westward at—

Trevone,

a growing holiday resort with post-office, new church, hotels, boarding-houses and bungalows. Trevone has made rapid progress in recent years and is now a separate ward in the Padstow Urban District. There is a sandy cove and a larger bay floored with cruel rocks; the seas here are fine when the wind is at all fresh, and surfing is popular. St. Saviours Church, recently built, is of local stone with Delabole slate roof. A regular bus service connects Trevone with Padstow.

Soon the forbidding rocky shore turns to the more smiling—

Harlyn Bay,

with a good sandy beach between headlands, a few houses and an hotel (*Lower Polmark*), near which is a *Museum* (*fee*), containing a number of antiquities excavated on the site.

In 1900 workmen sinking foundations for a house discovered several cists with human remains. These proved, on examination, to be late Celtic burials, which probably took place about 2,500 years ago. In all, upwards of 150 cists were found, the skeletons being all in the "crouched" position, laid on their left sides, and with heads towards the north. The remains were found beneath 10 to 15 feet of sand, which is supposed to have preserved them. This is one of the richest discoveries of prehistoric remains ever made in the British Isles.

Trevose Head and Lighthouse,

5 miles west of Padstow, should be visited. The walk can be taken either by way of Harlyn Bay and the cliffs, or by inland road to

St. Merryn (*Cornish Arms*), thence by a path which strikes a continuing road that goes almost direct to the Head or by other roads in the neighbourhood of Higher Harlyn. St. Merryn and the whole of this neighbourhood is popular with summer visitors. There is a golf course at Constantine Bay. In St. Merryn church (8, 11, 6) is the ancient font from the ruined church of St. Constantine. It is a beautiful specimen of fourteenth-century work, similar to that at Padstow.

Trevose Head is only 243 feet high, but the view along the coast is wonderful, past Bedruthan, Porth, Newquay, and even as far as St. Ives on a very clear day. The lighthouse can be inspected (*check times*). The headland is a fine mass of jagged rock, and the cliff scenery all round is grand and imposing. Cars may approach the headland *via* Trevose Farm but a toll is charged on entering the private road. The islets lying some way off are the **Quies Rocks.**

On the east side of Trevose Head is **Polventon Bay,** more commonly known as **Mother Ivey's Bay,** and beside Cataclews Point are the famous **Cataclews Quarries,** which have provided stone for many Cornish churches.

South of Trevose Lighthouse are several bays and coves. **Constantine Bay** provides a lovely stretch of sand (bathing, however, is dangerous, and great care should be taken, especially round about low tide).

Treyarnon Bay

is noteworthy for the extremely pleasant way in which it is being developed. There is a splendid beach providing perhaps the best surfing in Cornwall. **Porthcothan Bay,** three and a half miles from Trevose Head and five from Padstow has fine rock scenery on either hand—particularly on the south side of the bay. At the head of the bay are a few bungalows, and above the bridge carrying the road across the porth is a pretty green valley. Refreshments are obtainable. The ruins of **Constantine Church** are within half a mile of the sea at the bay of the same name and near the 18th tee of the Trevose golf links. Visitors wishing to see the ruins should inquire at the golf club-house. St. Constantine was a King of Cornwall, said to have been a descendant of Constantine the Great and the Empress Helena. There was, however, another Constantine, a chieftain converted by St. Petroc. This saint probably had a cell here. Hereabouts are many caverns, and at Porthcothan are several natural arches and caves, smuggling tales being told in connection with the latter. The cliff scenery is particularly fine.

The **Trevose Golf Links,** with a length of 6,667 yards over sea turf and sand dunes, were laid out by H. S. Colt. Recently, a number of chalets and cabins have been constructed for golfing and holiday accommodation. Full particulars from: Hon. Secretary, Trevose Golf Club, Constantine Bay, Padstow. Tel.: St. Merryn 208.

The famous **Bedruthan Steps** (*see* p. 45) lie 2 miles to the south, near to **Red Cliff Castle,** an ancient British camp.

St. Ervan and St. Eval are two parishes south of Padstow, somewhat off the usual route of tourists, but easily accessible in the course of the coast walk or from the Padstow–Newquay road. The tower of **St. Eval church,** which stands in a field away from the village, is very conspicuous. After destruction, it was rebuilt by Bristol merchants in 1727 as a day-mark. The north wall is Norman, and in it is an original window. Note the bench-ends and screens and Norman font. Registers date from 1695.

NORTHWARD FROM PADSTOW

Across the Camel from Padstow is the parish of **St. Minver,** with one or two noteworthy places on the coast. Particulars of the Padstow–Rock ferry are given on page 70. **Rock is a** popular sailing centre.

St. Enodoc Golf Links. This is one of the finest natural courses in England. The pavilion is at the southern end, approached by road from Rock, from which it is about five minutes distant. The length of the course is 6,050 yards. Sunday play. Particulars from: The Sec., St. Enodoc Golf Club, Rock, Wadebridge. Tel.: Trebetherick 3216.

The interesting little church of St. Michael (8, 11, 6), **Porthilly,** in a cove south of Rock, should be visited. At low tide it can be approached across the sands, from which it is reached by steps. The church was restored in 1865–7. Note the Norman font, the rood-screen frame, and tiny pulpit with linen-fold panelling. A tomb and a slab giving particulars of a charity are interesting, and outside the porch is a four-hole crosshead of some interest.

In the pretty mother village of—

St. Minver,

St. Menefreda's Church standing on the side of the valley, its spire visible for many miles, is well worth a visit (services at 8 and 11).

It contains an interesting slate monument with no date, but said to be that of Thomas Stone and wife (1604) and in the south aisle a brass to Roger Opy (1517). The Perpendicular font, magnificent bench-ends, and rood stairs are worthy of note. There are traces of Norman masonry in the chancel, and the north aisle has heavy octagonal pillars of flat stones, contrasting with the graceful granite monoliths on the south side. Against the west wall is a Norman Piscina found in 1927. The ancient stocks stand in the porch. The church plate includes a chalice of 1618. In the middle of a field in the parish of St. Minver Lowlands is **Jesus' Well,** but the chapel which stood near has disappeared during the last century.

A mile north of Rock, over the golf links, is the ancient **Church of St. Enodoc** (chapel of ease to St. Minver, 8, 3), which was threatened with the same fate as St. Piran-in-the-Sands. The sands did overwhelm the church, and the building at one time could only be entered through the roof, but happily it has been reclaimed and preserved. There are traces of Norman work and the font is of the same period. Note the holy water stoup at the south entrance, made into an almsbox, and the base of the fifteenth-century screen. The spire is slightly out of the perpendicular. The church overlooks delightful **Daymer Bay.**

The nearest way by road from Rock to St. Enodoc is to go along the Trebetherick road, until after a mile a public footpath with directions to the Church appears on the left.

A mile to the north, heading an inlet at the mouth of the Camel estuary is **Polzeath,** which seems to grow more popular year by year. It is more modern and sophisticated in appearance than most Cornish coves. On any fine day in the season the splendid sands present a gay scene of colourful activity, with bathers of all ages thoroughly enjoying themselves. Excellent surf-bathing. On either side are grand cliffs. There are a few shops, several bungalows, an extensive car park, tennis courts and a number of cafés. St. Enodoc Golf Club is within 2 miles. Old Polzeath lies at the head of the little inlet. Accommodation is available—*Lodge; Greystones;* etc.

On **Rumps Point,** to the north are ancient earthworks. Eastward is **Portquin Bay,** with magnificent scenery almost rivalling that of Tintagel. The village of **Portquin** lies in a tiny cove at the extreme east end of the Bay. At the junction of the Portquin–Port Isaac road is **Long Cross,** the shaft of an ancient cross with the inscription, "Brocagni hic jacet", probably referring to Brechan, a Welsh prince, and the father of St. Endelienta, the patron saint of the fifteenth-century **St. Endellion Church,** in the village of the same name. Note the holy water stoup, the south entrance, Norman font, bench-ends (recently replaced), carved wagon roofs, and unusual ball-topped pinnacles. The church also contains the handsome shrine of St. Endelienta.

Port Isaac

Early Closing Day.—Wednesday.
Licensing Hours.—10.30–2.30 and 5.30–10.30. Sundays, 12–2, 7–10.30.
Boats available for mackerel fishing.
Car Park.—Port Gaverne Road, and limited space at The Platt, near harbour;
Population.—1,000.

Distances.—Port Gaverne, ½ mile; Portquin, 2; St. Endellion, 2; Wadebridge, 9; Rock, 6; Polzeath, 5.

Hotels.—*Castle Rock; Lawns,* The Terrace; *Slipway House; Golden Lion; Tre-Pol-Pen.*

Port Isaac lies about 2 miles east of Portquin, from which it is reached by a path across the fields to the ancient farmhouse of Roscarrock, and then over hill and combe to the head of the inlet on which the fishing village is situated. The route by road is *via* Church Hill (1 in 5) or by way of St. Endellion. It is a delightfully quaint and old-world spot for a quiet holiday. Southern National buses connect with Wadebridge and with Bodmin Road on Western Region main line. For bathing it is advisable to go to Port Gaverne, boats may be hired for fishing, the golf links at Rock are handy, and the cliff walks are magnificent. On the hill-top are pleasant modern houses, but the oldest part of the port is packed so tightly between the steep hillsides that only with much difficulty can vehicles get into and out of the village. Motorists paying only a fleeting visit are strongly recommended to leave their cars up above and make their way down on foot.

Port Gaverne, close by, is a sheltered cove. It was at one time busy shipping slates and coal.

Just after passing through St. Endellion, on the Camelford road, the ancient mansion of **Tresungers** may be seen on the left of the valley. It is now a farmhouse, and has an embattled entrance tower of three stories, and bears the date 1660, when it was rebuilt. Portions of the older building remain.

Roscarrock, between Port Isaac and Portquin, was the seat of the ancient family of that name from the time of Richard I to 1673. There are several old mansions in this district.

Between 2 and 3 miles south-east of Port Isaac are the remains of **Tregeare Rounds** or **Castle Dameliock,** the "Castle Terrible" of the *Morte D'Arthur,* which Gorlois, the Duke of Cornwall, fortified against Uther-Pendragon. It lies to the right of the St. Endellion–Delabole road and consisted of three concentric ramparts, of which two remain with considerable portions of the outer ring.

At Delabole, a few miles farther from Port Isaac and about midway between Camelford and the coast, are the famous **Old Delabole Slate Quarries.** The slates from these quarries are noted particularly for their uniform colour and durability. In nearly all Cornish churches are memorial slabs and grave-stones made of Delabole slate, and even if many hundred years old, the inscriptions are plainly legible. John Wesley used to preach in the Delabole Quarry. Slate is still being quarried here.

The **De Lank Quarries,** which supplied the granite for the Eddystone Lighthouse, still supply stone. These lie on the edge of the Moors between Blisland and St. Breward.

WADEBRIDGE

Access.—Western Region main line train to Bodmin Road where connecting bus services maintained by the Western National Omnibus Company may be met.

Angling.—Salmon and trout angling may be obtained on the Camel and some of the other streams. Licences may be obtained from Paul's, Molesworth Street. The Wadebridge Angling Association issues short-period tickets for their waters.

Banks.—*Barclays, Lloyds, Midland, National Westminster,* all in Molesworth Street. *Trustee Savings,* The Platt.

Boating.—On the River Camel.

Bowls, Tennis and Putting at Egloshayle.

Buses.—To Rock, St. Enodoc, Polzeath and Port Isaac (all *via* St. Minver), to Newquay *via* St. Columb and St. Columb Road Station, to Bodmin, to Camelford, to Launceston, and to Tintagel (connecting with Bude and Bideford).

Car Park.—Cattle Market Annexe, Polmorla Road (free), Molesworth Street (free).

Cattle Market.—Mondays.

Cinema.—*Regal.*

Distances (Approximate); Tintagel, 16½; Boscastle, 17; Camelford, 11; Delabole, 13; Padstow, 8; Rock, 7; Port Isaac, 9; St. Mawgan, 12; Bedruthan, 12; Newquay, 16; St. Enodoc, 7; Trevone, 9; Trevose, 12; St. Columb, 8; Polzeath, 8.

Early Closing Day. Saturday.

Golf.—At Rock (*see* p. 78), or at Trevose (*see* p. 75).

Hotels.—*Molesworth Arms,* Molesworth St.; *Swan,* Molesworth Street; *Bridge on Wool,* The Platt; *The Rock,* Rock.

Licensing Hours.—11 to 2.30 and 5.30–11. Sundays, 12–2.30 and 7–10.30.

Places of Worship.—*St. Breock* and *Egloshayle churches; Methodist* and *Congregational* chapels. R.C. services at *St. Michael's.*

Population.—About 3,000.

Post Office.—The Platt, 9.00 a.m. to 5.30 p.m. Saturdays, 9–4.30.

Road Route from Newquay *via* St. Columb Minor and Major, where turn left on entering and descend hill (avoiding left-hand road half-way down). Road excellent to Wadebridge (16 miles).

Wadebridge stands at the head of the Camel estuary, about 8 miles from the sea—a clean and bright town, rapidly increasing in popularity. The river scenery, particularly above the town, is beautiful, the waters winding between wooded hills, the latter contrasting with the exposed hills seawards.

The name of the town is said to be derived from the Roman *Vadum*, a ford.

Owing to the swift-running *Camel* at this point, the ford was so dangerous that at one time, it is said, there was a chapel on each bank where travellers could pray for a safe crossing and offer up thanks on reaching the other side. About 1470, owing to the efforts of Thomas Loveybond, then vicar of Egloshayle, sufficient funds were raised to construct a much-needed bridge, but when the work commenced considerable difficulty was experienced in finding firm foundations for the piers. According to legend, the trouble was only overcome in the end by building these on wool-packs.

The **Bridge**, originally 510 feet long, of 17 pointed gothic arches, had angles over each pier as refuges for pedestrians against the traffic. Four of the original arches are now blocked up, three under the road at the town side and one beneath the eastern approach. In 1852-3 the bridge was widened three feet on each side by building granite segmental arches thrust out between the cutwaters. As this is, perhaps, the finest example in the British Isles of a 500-year-old bridge still in constant daily use great care was taken to preserve its appearance during a bridge widening scheme carried out in 1962-3.

On crossing the bridge and turning to the right **Egloshayle Church** will be reached in a little over half a mile, pleasantly placed overlooking river meadows.

This fine building was rebuilt by Loveybond at the same time the bridge was erected. St. Helie's coat of arms is one side of the door, that of the Kestell family on the other. The unplastered walls give the interior an unusually rugged appearance. There are two Celtic crosses by the south porch. The roof of the south aisle is well carved; there is a font of the Transition-Norman period, and a modern memorial screen in keeping with the beautiful pre-Reformation pulpit. The modern glass in the south aisle is remarkable for its lovely shades of blue and purple. In the base of the fine tower— said to have been built of stone left over from the bridge—are remains of a monument to the Kestell family, bearing dates from 1520 to 1581. The registers date from 1600.

St. Breock Church (St. Brioc), a mile west of the town, and beautifully situated, with a stream running through the churchyard, contains portions of a thirteenth-century building. The tower dates from this period. The two doorways and the two windows at the west end of the nave are fourteenth-century while the font and the two windows in the south aisle date from the fifteenth century. The walls are bare of plaster and the nave is long, unbroken by a screen and enclosed chancel, so that a fine view is obtained of the beautiful alabaster reredos. Of the various memorials the oldest (a priest's tomb), at the east end, is early thirteenth-century. There are one or two brasses of much interest, but most tourists versed in Cornish legend and story will be more interested in the slab inscribed "Here lyeth buryed John Tregeagle of Trevorder, Esq.", the year being 1679. This commemorates the son of Jan Tregeagle whose never-ending task it was to empty Dozmary Pool with a leaky limpet shell (*see* p. 89). The tombstone is among others at the east end of the south aisle. Jan's own tombstone has never been found although his burial in 1655 is recorded in the church register.

Coronation Park (in commemoration of King Edward VII's accession), on the **St. Breock** side, is a very lovely natural woodland on the slopes of the Polmorla valley. There are pleasant paths and numerous seats and in the early summer the scene is bright and gay with primroses and bluebells. In the only open space, at the top of the hill, is the town's War Memorial. On the Egloshayle side of the river is a large playing field with facilities for tennis, boating, cricket, football, bowls, net-ball, putting, etc. There is also a car park.

Good boating can be enjoyed at Wadebridge, and the river scenery is very picturesque. **Polbrock** and **Grogley,** with their woods, are favourite spots for rambles. The walk by way of Washaway (Bodmin bus route) is of great interest: Slades-bridge, a mile beyond Egloshayle, is charming with an old bridge (recently widened) and old mill. The little church of St. Conan, about two miles farther, and a little west of Washaway, has a Saxon font. There is a wayside cross, known as the **Prior's Cross,** on which are *fleurs-de-lys,* resembling the Prince of Wales' Feathers.

At **Nanscow,** about 2 miles south-west of Wadebridge, is to be seen the tombstone, supposed to be 1,200 years old, of Ulcagnus, son of Severus. From the stone stile at west end of St. Breock church take footpath (left) up to road; follow road (not field lane) a short distance to a path (left) crossing fields to a bridle path between trees. Continue down to open ground until Nanscow comes into sight on the left. This walk might be continued to the fine cromlech known as the **Giant's Quoit,** near Pawton. A picturesque short cut to the road in the valley will be pointed out by the courteous farm people of Nanscow. Turn right and take the somewhat steep road to the left farther on, which eventually comes out by a farm, where, if available, a guide will show the Cromlech. It stands in the middle of a cultivated field, so cannot always be approached. On these **St. Breock Downs** are other stones of archæological interest, including another cromlech, known by various names, but as the ground is largely enclosed they are not always easy to find. The views are extensive, especially that from the highest point, the **Beacon** (739 feet). The local branch of the Old Cornwall Society hold here their bonfire ceremony on Midsummer's Eve.

The somewhat roundabout road from Wadebridge to Padstow, 8 miles, has several interesting views of the Camel estuary. The village of **St. Issey** calls for little attention, but the church has a fine west doorway ; note also the restored fifteenth-century stone reredos, and late Norman font.

Little Petherick is charmingly placed at the head of **Petherick Creek,** an inlet on the Camel estuary.

The fourteenth-century church was practically rebuilt in 1858 and is a veritable museum of ecclesiastical treasures. A priest's tombstone, one of only three of its type in Cornwall, and formerly used as a doorstep, can be seen between the altars. There is a magnificent carved and gilded screen, worked by a local craftsman. The reredos on the Lady altar was erected in memory of the rector, during whose incumbency the restoration was undertaken, while that on the High Altar has more recently been added to the memory of his successor. The bench-ends—only three of which are original—were carved by a Belgian refugee. A Norman font, packhorse bells, an ancient inn clock, a Venetian processional cross and Byzantine altar cross and a pair of procession lanterns, are among the other treasures of this beautiful church. In the vestry is one of the finest collections of vestments in Cornwall.

Some few miles eastward of Wadebridge and reached by a turning from the Camelford road at St. Kew Highway (the railway over the road is closed) is the pretty little village of—

St. Kew,

in its beautiful wooded vale. One of the most picturesque villages of the district, it is chiefly visited on account of its interesting church.

Beautifully plain, without plaster, its attractions include the windows of rare old painted glass. One, in the north chapel, dating from about 1469, depicts our Lord's Passion; over this window are the arms of Henry V, for in mediaeval times there was a King's Chapel and priest at St. Kew. In the south chapel are the fragments of a Jesse window, which experts date at about 1350. There is also some old glass in one or two windows in the aisle. All of the old roof timbers and four bench-ends remain; the modern screen incorporates a portion of the original, and the pulpit is Elizabethan. Note the coloured plaster Royal Arms (1661) with a fearsome lion and "God Save the King," and the ringers' rhyme-board in the base of the tower. There are also stocks, a Cornish cross, by the church steps, a rare fifteenth-century lantern cross, and an interesting old almsbox, while the "Ogham" stone inscribed IUSTI is probably fifth century. The ogham writing of the Gaels consists of combinations of straight lines, which are seen on the edge of the stone.

Two miles out of Wadebridge on the Camelford road is **Three Holes Cross** from where a farm track going due east arrives in ½-mile at **Castle Killibury** or **Kelly Rounds,** a prehistoric hill fort and possibly the original Killiwick of Arthurian romance. It was certainly a place of considerable importance and is notable now for the remarkable range of view it offers: St. Minver's spire, St. Endellion's tower, Rough Tor and Brown Willy and other landmarks from east to west.

At the north-east end of the parish close to the road to Delabole from Pendoggett is a fine example of an Iron Age fort, known as **Tregeare Rounds,** consisting of double ramparts and ditches. This is thought by some to be the Damelioc of the Arthurian legend.

King Arthur's Country

Camelford—Tintagel—Boscastle

Camelford, Tintagel and Boscastle, stand at the three points of a triangle. Tintagel and Boscastle are on the coast, about 3 miles apart, while Camelford is situated, on the main Wade-bridge–Bude road, about 4 miles inland, about equidistant from the two places on the coast. There are coach excursions to Tintagel and Boscastle daily in the summer from Newquay, Bude, and almost every resort in Cornwall. Buses now replace the former railway connection to Camelford, while the whole district is very popular with motorists. The neighbourhood is closely associated with the Arthurian legends, and therefore of the greatest attraction to visitors interested in literature and romance.

CAMELFORD

Approaches.—Western Region line to Okehampton, thence by road. **Road Routes.**—On main road from North Devon to Land's End (A39).
Air Services with coach connection via Newquay Airport.
Banks.—*Barclays, Lloyds, National Westminster, Midland* with agencies at Boscastle, Tintagel and Delabole.
Buses.—To Wadebridge, St. Columb and Newquay; Trewarmett and Trebarwith; Tintagel, Boscastle, Bude, etc.; Launceston and Port Isaac.
Car Parking.—Free, by Town Hall, "The Clease", and Church Field.
Churches.—The old parish church is at Lanteglos, off the Wadebridge road. A new church, dedicated to St. Thomas, has been built in Camelford itself. It is interesting as a modern church built with local material—Delabole stone with a Delabole rustic slate roof. Three Methodist churches.
Early Closing.—Wednesday.
Fishing.—Licences for trout and salmon at Council Offices, Camelford. Good sea fishing.
Hotels.—*Sunnyside; Highermead.*
Licensing Hours.—10.30–2.30; 5.30–11. Sundays 12–2, 7–10.30.
Market Day.—Thursday (first of month)
Hunting.—The North Cornwall Hunt.
Population.—Approx. 2,000. 7,577 Rural District.

Camelford, the "Camelot" of Tennyson, lies four miles inland from the coast, on the banks of the river Camel. Leland calls the place *Kamblen* and Camden *Gaffelford*, which latter identifies it with Arthur's last battle.

85

It is a small and ancient town, quaint and quiet—except for the traffic—and was made a free borough in 1259. The insignia of the extinct corporation are very interesting. The mace was a gift in 1660.

Formerly Camelford sent two members to Parliament. Among its representatives were James Macpherson, of Ossian's poems fame, and Lord Brougham. It is recorded that from 1812 to 1818 the members paid the patron £8,000 for their seats, and on another occasion as much as £6,000 was paid in bribes.

At **Slaughter Bridge,** a good mile above the town, legend says the armies of King Arthur and his nephew, Mordred the Usurper, met in 542. Mordred was killed, and the King mortally wounded. The Bridge should be seen from the low ground by the stream, when its antiquity will be apparent. It somewhat resembles the clapper bridges on Dartmoor.

Near it, in a beautiful and secluded glen known as *Worthyvale*, will be found the spot known as **King Arthur's Grave,** though he is generally believed to have been buried at Glastonbury. The story is that the body rested here for three days. The stone that marks the spot was formerly used as a bridge, but many years ago was set up by the Dowager Lady Falmouth, and now lies actually in the stream itself. Permission to see the stone and the Manor of Worthyvale, in whose grounds it lies, is obtained by making application at the beautiful old house which lies several hundred yards up the lane turning off from the main road close to the bridge on the station side. The lane is marked by two granite posts (one broken), and further down the lane, is a weatherbeaten sign which says "To the stone" and if followed, brings one to the stream.

In recent years Camelford has developed as a holiday centre. Its attractions include a fine bracing air coming from the sea on one side and from moorland on the other; convenient access to Boscastle, Tintagel, Brown Willy, and Rough Tor; numerous prehistoric remains on the moor; interesting churches; fine sands at Trebarwith ($4\frac{1}{4}$ miles); and trout-fishing in the Camel and other streams. Quaint corners attract photographers and artists. During the summer, coaches run to places of interest around and buses bring the coast and the beautiful valley of the *Allen*, on the verge of the moors, within easy reach. As a moorland resort, Camelford has great possibilities.

Excursions from Camelford

A pleasant excursion can be made to the little hamlet of **Lanteglos-by-Camelford** (not to be confused with Lanteglos-by-Fowey), about a mile to the south. Few people who stay any time in the locality fail to visit Lanteglos church, which is the mother church of Camelford. It is beautifully situated amid trees. The church has traces of Norman masonry. The fine tower was erected in the fifteenth century, and the font is of the same period. Note the round-headed sedilia in the chancel and fifteenth-century glass showing Christ and His Apostles in the upper lights of the aisle windows; also the top of a round-headed cross and remains of stone tracery preserved at the west end of the church, and the tombstone dated 1560. In the churchyard are four old crosses and an ancient Saxon pillar stone found at Castle Goff in 1876.

At **Castle Goff,** a little west of Lanteglos church, are ancient fortifications. The road which encircles the church, turning up at the S.E. corner of the graveyard, leads to the hamlet of **Helstone,** which proudly claims to be the place referred to in the Domesday records as having forty brewers!

A passage through an archway in the main street beneath decorators' premises leads to a path beside and over the stream. About 2 miles southward by this path is **Advent Parish Church** (St. Adwenna), containing a circular Norman font and some ancient memorials. The tall unbuttressed tower, granite arcade and north windows are fourteenth-century, and porch and wagon roofs, beautifully carved, are late fifteenth century. A mile farther south is the **Devil's Jump,** two huge piles of granite one on either side of a deep ravine. It is a weird spot, and many are the legends told of it. The whole district of Camelford, indeed, is rich in antiquities and ancient lore. On the Tresinney estate is an ancient cross with shaft 6 feet 9 inches high.

Advent Church can be reached by car by taking the main road to Bodmin from Camelford for approximately 3 miles then turning left where signposted. This is a narrow but scenic drive past a picturesque but now disused mill on the River Camel.

St. Teath, south of Camelford, 2 miles beyond Helstone and just off the main road, has an ancient church rebuilt on a Norman fabric in the fifteenth century. The pulpit is dated 1630. Note the Carminow arms in the centre panel with the Cornish motto:

"Cala: Rag: Whetlow "; "A straw for a talebearer."

Over a doorway in the tower is a similar date, but this only refers to the doorway itself. There are numerous memorials within the building, some fine bench-ends and a fifteenth-century greenstone font. In the churchyard annexe is a fine old cross, 13 feet high, the second highest in the county.

Warbstow Bury is an enormous ringed defensive earthwork with a sepulchral mound in the centre. It is about 4 miles from Davidstow and is 800 feet up.

Along the valley of the Camel, which is roughly followed by the Camelford–Bodmin road, are many interesting villages with picturesque churches and cottages. The valley forms the western side of the moors, so that, with the exception of St. Breward and Blisland (which is described in connection with Bodmin) most of the villages are on the western side of the valley. They are too numerous to be described categorically, but here are notes on a few of them.

Michaelstow is reached by turning to the right from the Camelford–Bodmin road (B3266) about 2¼ miles from the Wadebridge fork. The church lies at the back of a pleasant chained green, and, with a magnificent cross, a well in the churchyard, a stone porch with narrow arch, Tudor doorway, octagonal font and handsome bench-ends, is beautiful in itself and is set in lovely surroundings.

St. Breward is reached by a poor but picturesque road which turns left from B3266, half a mile beyond Michaelstow. The church has traces of five circular Norman pillars on the north side, made of large slabs of granite, while the south pillars are fluted, with a flat arch.

It makes a pleasant round to continue from St. Breward through **Row** and **Lank** (near the De Lank quarries), to cross the Camel again at Wenford bridge, with china clay works a mile to the south, and to climb up to **St. Tudy** (*Cornish Arms*). This is a pretty, open village with a little green in front of the church, which has some old monuments, a Transition font and very fine carved work in the porch. One of its most interesting features is the coped stone, one of only 30 in England, of possible Norse origin which was found deeply buried in the churchyard and now, with explanatory notes, is carefully preserved in the porch.

From St. Tudy the Bodmin road may be regained and return made direct to Camelford. It is more interesting, however, to continue southward for rather less than two miles and turn to the right at Longstone cross-roads, reaching **St. Mabyn** in another mile.

From St. Mabyn continue down a steep hill to cross the river Allen, emerging on to the Camelford–Wadebridge road just near St. Kew Highway.

Brown Willy and Rough Tor

The moors of Cornwall are neither so extensive nor so high as Dartmoor, but they have many features in common with the Devonshire moors, together with a fine, bracing air. The hunter of stone-circles and prehistoric dwellings may make sure of finding a good appetite as well as archæological remains. But in wet weather the moors become almost impassable for strangers unacquainted with their paths, and at all ordinary times those unaccustomed to such open tracts must beware of the bogs and avoid short cuts across lower-lying ground

TINTAGEL, BOSCASTLE, CAMELFORD

English Miles

0   1   2   3   4

WARD, LOCK & CO. LIMITED, LONDON

© John Bartholomew & Son Ltd, Edinburgh

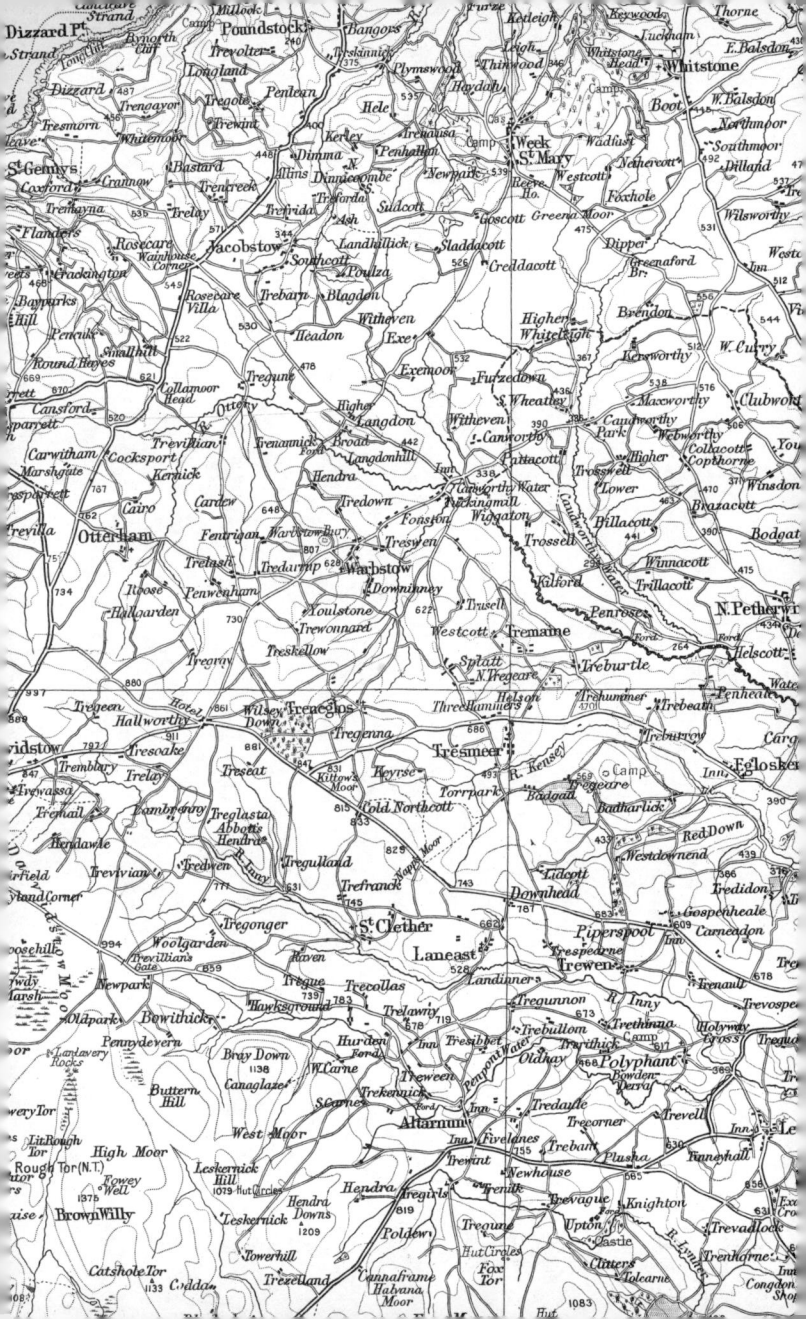

traversed by streams. Bus routes now practically encircle the Cornish moors, and one crosses the centre, so that the walker can easily plan expeditions. **Brown Willy,** 1,375 feet high (the highest point in Cornwall), and its near neighbour, **Rough Tor** (pronounced like bough), 1,312 feet high, are the two principal heights. The scenery is wildly grand, rugged and bleak. At the summit of Rough Tor (N.T.) are some magnificent piled rocks.

To reach Rough Tor and Brown Willy from Camelford town, go over the bridge and in a few minutes bear off on the right along the ascending road leading almost straight to the heights. This is the Jubilee Road which goes to within three-quarters of a mile of the summit. It is accessible to cars but is rough at the far end. The path onward is clear but in wet weather becomes difficult. Rough Tor is first reached. Brown Willy is a mile and a quarter beyond. The bog between them should be carefully noted and avoided. The distance from Camelford is about 5 miles. The return can be pleasantly varied by walking on from Brown Willy to the Bodmin–Launceston road, there getting a bus to Bodmin and so back to Camelford. The main road is struck not far from Bolventor (*Jamaica Inn*), opposite which a good road leads in about 2 miles to—

Dozmary Pool

There is little in the scenery of the pool to justify the excursion, but by reason of its association with the Arthurian legends it is visited by considerable numbers, for here took place the traditional passing of Arthur and the return to the mystic giver of his invincible sword *Excalibur*.

From a paper signed John Gatcombe and dated 1873, reproduced in *Notes and Queries*, the following is extracted:

"The formation of such a body of water on high ground is considered singular and curious. There is a popular legend attached to this pool, which is this: that a person named Tregeagle, rich and powerful, but very wicked, guilty of murder and other heinous crimes, lived near this place, and that after his death his spirit haunted the neighbourhood, but was at length exorcised and laid to rest in Dozmary Pool; but having in his life-time disposed of his soul and body to the wicked one, his infernal majesty takes great pleasure in tormenting him by imposing on him difficult tasks, such as spinning a rope with sand, and dipping out the pool with a limpet-shell with a hole in the bottom, etc., and at times amuses himself with hunting him over the moors with his hell-hounds, at which time Tregeagle is heard to howl and roar in a most dreadful manner, so that 'roaring and howling like Tregeagle' is a not uncommon expression amongst the people

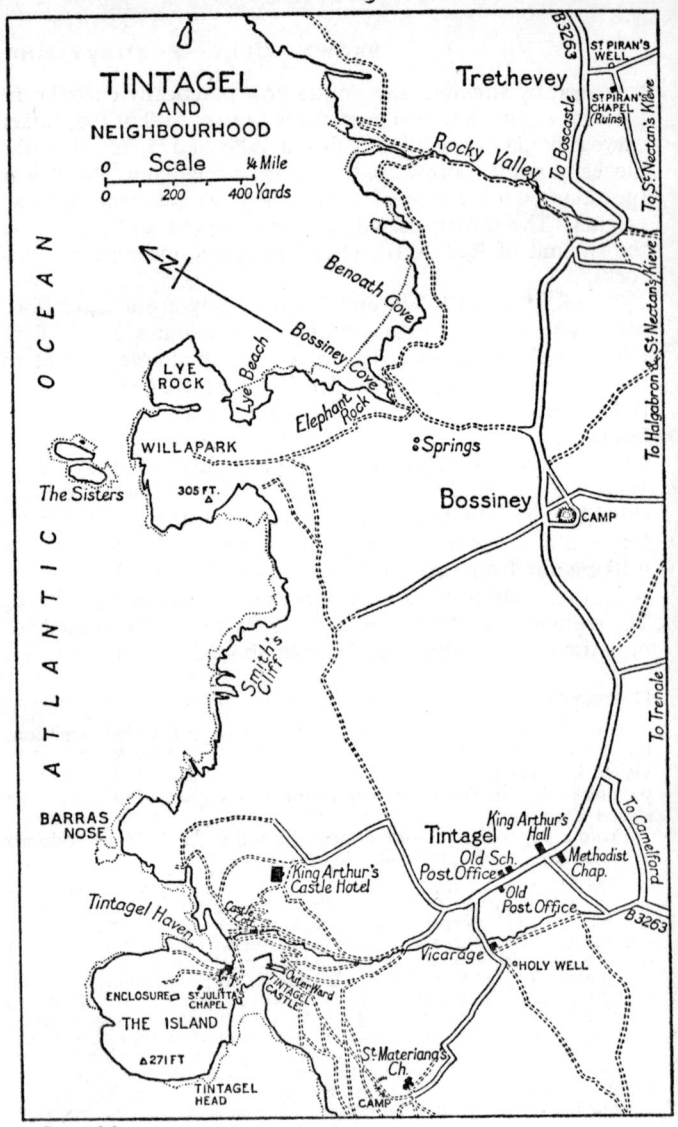

TINTAGEL
AND
NEIGHBOURHOOD

Scale ¼ Mile

0   200   400 Yards

ATLANTIC OCEAN

Trethevey

St PIRAN'S WELL

St PIRAN'S CHAPEL (Ruins)

To Boscastle

To St Nectan's Kieve

Rocky Valley

Benoath Cove

Bossiney Cove

LYE ROCK

Lye Beach

WILLAPARK

The Sisters

305 FT.

Elephant Rock

Springs

Bossiney

CAMP

To Halgabron & St Nectan's Kieve

To Trenale

Smith's Cliffs

BARRAS NOSE

King Arthur's Hall

Tintagel

Old Sch.

Post Office

Methodist Chap.

Old Post Office

King Arthur's Castle Hotel

To Camelford

B 3263

Tintagel Haven

Cast.

Vicarage

HOLY WELL

ENCLOSURE

St JULITTA CHAPEL

THE ISLAND

Outer Ward

TINTAGEL CASTLE

271 FT.

St Materiana's Ch.

TINTAGEL HEAD

CAMP

Copyright]

90

of Cornwall; indeed, many would not go near the place after dark for the world.

"I have an idea that the supposed noise of the hell-hounds might be caused by the flights of wild geese over the moor at night."

There was a story that Dozmary was bottomless. But the pool dried up in 1869 and so disposed of that legend. With regard to Tennyson's story of *Excalibur*, it is said by some that the poet pictured the event as happening at Looe Pool, near Helston, which better answers to the scene described in *Morte d'Arthur*.

Refreshments can be obtained near the Pool.

In the neighbourhood is **Hawk's Tor** (1,006 ft.), on the south-eastern slope of which are the famous **Stripple Stones.** Sir Norman Lockyer, by taking the alignment through the north-east bastion to the star Capella, dated the erection of this circle as 1250 B.C. This is the only Cornish circle to resemble Stonehenge and Avebury in being surrounded by a circular ditch and bank. There were originally 28 stones, the tallest of them 13 feet high.

TINTAGEL

Approaches.—(*a*) By rail to Okehampton thence by bus, 40 miles; (*b*) by bus from Bude, Camelford or Wadebridge. Coaches from all parts of Cornwall.

Banks.—*Barclays, Lloyds, Midland, National Westminster.* (Agencies.)

Bathing.—At Bossiney Cove, Benoath, Tintagel Cove and Trebarwith Strand.

Buses.—To Boscastle and Bude, to Camelford and Wadebridge. Coaches make excursions to places of interest during the season.

Car Parks are numerous.

Distances (approximate).—Camelford, 5; Bodmin, 20 ; Boscastle, 3½; Trebarwith Strand, 2; Wadebridge, 16½; Launceston, 21; Bude, 18½; St. Nectan's Kieve, 1½.

Early Closing Day.—Wednesday.

Hotels.—*Wharncliffe Arms; Tintagel; Atlantic View* (private)*; Mill House Inn; King Arthur's Castle; Rocky Valley.*

Licensing Hours.—10.30–2.30 and 5.30–11. Sundays, 12–2, 7–10.30.

Places of Worship, with hours of Sunday services: *St. Materiana* (Parish Church) —8, 11 and 6. *Methodist,* at Trevena and Trewarmett—11 and 6. Bossiney—11 and 6. *Holy Family,* Treknow, 9.30. *St. Piran,* Trethevy, 7.30. *Roman Catholic,* St. Paul The Apostle, 10.

Population.—1,300.

Road Routes.—*See* pp. 6–9.

Youth Hostel at Dunderhole Point.

Museum.—Shell and coin collection Fore Street.

Visitors to the village which they imagine to be Tintagel are often surprised to discover that its name is actually **Trevena.** The explanation is that Tintagel is a parish, containing the village of Trevena. As a village, none could at first sight be less interesting. A long, winding street, a miscellaneous collection of quite unattractive modern houses and rather bleak scenery, are not exactly the features of the Tintagel of our imaginations, though there are some delightful old grey stone

buildings. This, however, is quite immaterial, as the castle itself which stands quite apart from the village, is the real object of the pilgrimage.

Tintagel, some 300 feet above the sea, has, however, a charm and majesty which grows on acquaintance. The air is most invigorating, whilst the cliff walks disclose some of the most magnificent scenery in Great Britain.

There is bathing at Bossiney (best near low or half-tide, as the beach is not large), and during the summer coaches make long and short excursions to places of interest.

Tintagel, jointly with Bossiney, was once a borough and sent two representatives to the House of Commons. Sir Francis Drake and, later, Sir Francis Cotton, secretary to Prince Charles, afterwards Charles I, were the most illustrious of these. The Corporation mace, seal, etc., are preserved.

On the left of the road leading through the village is the **Old Post Office,** an interesting old building built originally as a medieval manor house and dating from the fourteenth century, and now cared for by the National Trust. Open Mar.–Oct. 10–1, 2–6; also Suns. May–Sept. 2–6. Dec.–Feb., key from caretaker. Closed Nov. *Charge.*

For Tintagel Castle and Cove (about a third of a mile distant) take the second lane on left, where the road bears sharply to right, near the end of the village. The way down is clearly indicated. The lane is impracticable for cars, but there are several parks close to hand. The little stream to the left of the path which, in summer, quietly meanders down to the sea, is transformed in winter into a rushing torrent culminating in a magnificent waterfall which pours tons of water on to the beach every minute. Heavy rains in summer produce a like effect.

At the second little stone-slab bridge on the left will be seen a notice "To Lower Ward". Disregarding this for the time being we continue down the main path towards—

Tintagel Castle

Admission.—The Ministry of Public Building and Works makes a small charge. Children and organised parties at reduced rate. Official Guide books at Custodian's Office.

Open: May–September, daily, 9.30–7. March, April, October: 9.30–5.30, Sundays, 2–5.30; November to February, 9.30–4, Sundays, 2–4.

On arriving at the Cove a few yards after passing the Café on the right and the Custodian's office on the left, the **Beach** of dark sand and slaty pebbles is seen below, with the vast mass of **Tintagel Head** towering above to the left. To descend to the beach follow the path to the left for a few yards when the steps will be seen on the right. There is also a less secure way down on the right.

Gazing upwards from the beach the wild and rugged grandeur of the great headland (rising to some 270 ft.) is impressive in the extreme—without doubt an ideal site for a medieval fortress. At the base and piercing the great cliff is **Merlin's Cave**, through which access is gained to the miniature beach on the south side of the headland, if the tide is low. It is advisable to make sure that the water is still receding before venturing through.

Tintagel Head is connected to the mainland by a short, narrow isthmus, but is likely to become an island before many years have passed. Already it is referred to locally as such. In 1820, and again in 1846, great masses of cliff fell away, leaving the remains of the Castle precariously clinging to the very edge of the headland. Hereabouts was the site of the ancient **Drawbridge.**

The Castle site was explored and various excavations made by the Ministry of Works in 1933–6. Their conclusions were that the Castle dates from the twelfth century and that, prior to that time, a Celtic religious settlement existed on the headland.

To visit the ruins of the **Norman Stronghold,** so rich in legend and romance, commence the ascent by the winding foot-path (beyond the steps leading down to the beach) and cross the "Bridge" over the isthmus which leads up steeply, by steps and railing, to the **Entrance Door.** Those who make the effort will be amply rewarded by the magnificent views in all directions, with the added interest and satisfaction of visiting what is left of one of the most romantic strongholds of ancient times.

The date over the entrance (1852) refers to the year when the Castle was first opened to the public. This doorway gives access to **The Precincts.** The large structure on the right is known as the **Norman Hall,** inside which is a smaller building some 12 ft. high. The latter is said to date from the fourteenth century and is believed to have been used for the safe keeping of State prisoners. The scattered ruins of the twelfth-century fortifications, fragments of buildings and some stone steps of a winding stairway are seen on the right. It is possible to trace the area of **The Courtyard** and to follow the curtain of **Battlements,** at least for some of their length. Like the **Iron**

Gate (a one-time fortified landing-place) this Curtain is believed to date from the thirteenth century. On the Plateau forming the centre of the "island" are the remains of the **Chapel of St. Julitta,** probably a Norman building, around which can be traced the outline of still earlier enclosures. Beyond, may be seen the **Castle Well** and a rectangular enclosure, the remains of what is believed to have been a medieval garden.

What is left of the **Lower Ward** on the mainland (referred to in an earlier paragraph), can be reached by the steps opposite the Island or the steep path which begins by the side of the Custodian's Office. A small charge is made to visit these outer ruins. An easier path begins at the village, and has already been referred to. By continuing the ascent to the top a grand view of the Headland is obtained while **The Church** is within a short distance on more or less level ground to the south.

However fragmentary, these ancient remains, so romantically situated, are truly awe-inspiring. The tremendous cliffs, the ruins, the glamour of poetry and romance, combine to make an indelible impression. Tintagel presents the most majestic cliff scenery in Cornwall. All the cliffs around seem castellated—Nature's own works of fortification—and it is difficult to say where walls begin and rocks end.

Everyone is so familiar with the Arthurian legend, either from the pages of *Morte d'Arthur* or from Tennyson, that it need not be outlined here. Dozmary Pool, away on Bodmin Moors beyond Bolventor, is generally accepted as the scene of the final disappearance of the famous sword *Excalibur*, but some contend that Looe Pool, near Helston, in the Lizard district, is the more likely place. Dozmary is no longer difficult of access, and the route is given on p. 89.

The earliest remains at Tintagel are those of the Celtic monastery, dating between the fifth and ninth centuries and already in ruins when the Castle was built. The Great Hall and Chapel were erected by Reginald, Earl of Cornwall, at the time when Tintagel is first mentioned by Geoffrey of Monmouth (1141–75).

Tintagel was then alienated and only recovered by Richard, the brother of Henry III, in 1235. He increased the strength of the Castle, building the Outer Ward on the mainland and the Curtain enclosing the courtyard and the iron gate covering the seaward approach on the island. In 1245 David, Prince of North Wales, was the guest, at Tintagel, of Richard, Earl of Cornwall, King of the Romans. Several governors were appointed but the dilapidations of time received no attention from them. In fact, about the year 1330, John, Earl of Cornwall, caused the great hall, which was partly in ruins, to be demolished. Subsequently this royal residence became a prison in charge of a constable, and numbered among its prisoners one John of Northampton, Lord Mayor of London. The early historians of the county, Leland, Carew, and others, all refer to the castle as being in complete ruin in the middle of the sixteenth century. Leland records that between the present Outer Ward and the Castle some long elm trees were placed across the chasm to form a bridge. Since those days the distance between the two cliffs has become more pronounced, owing to the action of the weather. The Prince Consort revived the honorary office of Constable, or Governor, of the Castle.

The whole site is under the control of the Ministry of Works, and extensive excavations have been carried out by Mr. Ralegh Radford, the Celtic authority, who has written an interesting and informative handbook, giving an account of the work and the history of the site. He concludes that Geoffrey of Monmouth, who undoubtedly used his authorities freely, made Tintagel the setting of the Arthurian legend rather because of its beauty and suitability for its purpose than from any definite data. Though Arthur was an historical figure, nothing has been found during the excavations to give archæological support to any special connection with Tintagel, but the mere fact that it has been for so many centuries the traditional centre of the legend adds a glowing mantle of romance to its inherent and very individual natural charm.

Before leaving Tintagel a visit should be paid to—

King Arthur's Hall

Open (weekdays only) during season, from 9 a.m. Tickets of admission (*small charge*) may be obtained from the counter in the entrance hall, where a comprehensive library of Arthurian literature is displayed.

The Hall, which was built by the late Mr. F. T. Glasscock as the headquarters of the Fellowship of the Round Table, is constructed entirely of Cornish stone, a great part of which was raised in Tintagel, and it is large enough to accommodate a thousand people. Quarrying has always been one of the chief industries of Cornishmen and a marvellous variety of stones is to be found in the county; in fact over fifty different kinds have been used in this building. These range from granite and slate to the rarer stones such as serpentine, porphyry, tourmaline, and greenstone.

There are no doors in the body of the Hall, which, simply but beautifully furnished, is one of the loveliest modern stone buildings in England. Open arches lead to a corridor which surrounds the whole building. In the Hall and the corridor are seventy-three windows, decorated with modern British stained glass. Those in the Hall represent episodes in the history of the Round Table and the Quest of the Sangrael, and, symbolically, the virtues of Knighthood; those in the corridor portray the arms of the Knights. At one end of the Hall granite steps lead up to a granite throne, above which is a large block of granite supported by pillars of different varieties of the same rock. Upon this rests a stone with an anvil into which is set a sword, representing the test which the youthful Arthur successfully passed and so proved his right of kingship over all the ambitious aspirants to the throne.

According to Malory, the stone was found near the high altar of the greatest church of London, and it is described as "a great stone four square, like unto a marble stone, and in midst thereof was like an anvil of steel a foot on high, and therein stuck a fair sword naked by the point, and letters there were written in gold about the sword that said thus: 'Whoso pulleth out this sword of this stone and anvil, is rightwise king born of all England.'"

The stone upon which the anvil and sword are set is of special interest as it was found near an ancient Celtic burial-place. It was moved to its present position without even removing the lichen which was growing upon it.

Before the throne is a Round Table of granite, and at the other end of the Hall is one of oak. There is an interesting collection of ancient manuscripts and a library of Arthurian literature which is probably the most complete in the world.

This Hall was officially opened on June 5, 1933. An older Hall is also shown. It is furnished with thrones, and a Round Table, and decorated with banners and weapons of Knighthood. Upon the walls are oil paintings by the late William Hatherall, R.I. The bjects of these are scenes from Malory's *Morte d'Arthur*.

After passing the Old Post Office, the first turn to the left will take one to the church, passing the Vicarage at the bottom of the hill. At the Vicarage some relics of the Castle are plainly visible from the road. The most interesting is the thirteenth- or fourteenth-century arch leading into the former coach-house, now a lovely little Chapel. In the garden is a large Norman columbarium; also the remains of rectangular fish ponds. Continuing up the other side of the valley, the road reaches—

The Church of St. Materiana

perched on the top of the cliffs overlooking Tintagel "island" and to be seen for miles around. This is a terribly exposed position; even the tombstones have to be buttressed against the fury of Atlantic gales. Within, the church, with its impressive gloom, is strangely peaceful in contrast. It is unusually interesting, even for a Cornish church, and this in spite of a careful but over-thorough "restoration" in 1870. The carved font is Norman, and is described by Dr. Cox in his *Churches of Cornwall* as "unique". The south doorway is Norman, while the north doorway has several Saxon features. There is a well-preserved medieval stone altar in the Lady chapel. A milestone, found some years ago, bearing an inscription which may refer to the Emperor Licinius, the brother-in-law of Constantine the Great, is in the south transept. Note the mutilated fifteenth-century rood screen; also the thirteenth-century memorial slab on the floor near the lectern. The brass effigy is fifteenth-century. The outside ironwork of the north door is noteworthy; the hinges are Early English, thought to date from about 1225.

Excursions from Tintagel

To Boscastle. By road, about three and a half miles, crossing the Rocky Valley. In dry weather the cliff path should be taken, starting from the *King Arthur's Castle Hotel*, reached by following the road to the right instead of turning down the path to the Castle. It is longer than by the road; the path crosses the Rocky Valley by a footbridge, but the scenery here is magnificent. For Boscastle *see* p. 100.

Trebarwith Strand. This charming spot, popular for picnicking and bathing, may be reached *via* Treknow or by footpath. It is one and a half miles south of Tintagel. The approach by road is romantic, running down between steep hillsides littered with quarry debris and thickly clothed with bracken, heather, and numerous wild flowers. The strand is nearly a mile long at low tide, and there is hotel accommodation. The vast walls of cliff, the caves, sands, and sea, with the Gull Rock conspicuous in the distance, make a fine scene. The bathing and surfing are excellent, except at high tide.

St. Nectan's Kieve and the **Rocky Valley.** A visit here should on no account be omitted, for such beautiful sylvan scenery is wholly unsuspected so close to wild Tintagel. Follow road past King Arthur's Hall (avoiding turn to right), soon passing through Bossiney (*see* below). The road then descends steeply (1 in 9) to a bridge crossing a stream.

(*a*) On the left at the approach to the bridge is a farm-gate which is the entrance to the public path going down the **Rocky Valley,** the haunt of the raven. The scenery is extremely beautiful, with huge rocks, trees, ferns, wild flowers, and a noisy brook. Half-way down is a ruined mill where on the rock face are carved two mazes or cabalistic signs which may have some early magical signficance. They are thought to be Bronze Age.

(*b*) Perhaps the pleasantest route to the Kieve and Waterfall is through the fields, turning off to the right over a stile by a farmyard at the beginning of Bossiney. The path leads through another farm, crosses the road and descends to the thickly-wooded valley. There are direction-boards pointing to the Kieve. Admission to the Waterfall is obtained from the *Hermitage* (*Tea Garden*). The height of the cascade is forty feet, the greater part of which is a sheer drop; the water then rushes through a natural arch to a shorter fall. The return can be made by lane over the hill, from which wide spreading views may be obtained. Coloured discs make the way easy to find.

An alternative route is by the lane which goes up beside the *Rocky Valley Hotel* and passes St. Piran's Chapel.

St. Knighton, or Nectan, was a brother of St. Morwenna (Morwenstow), and had also cells at Welcombe and Hartland, where he died about the sixth century.

Bossiney,

Hotel.—*Bossiney House* (with tennis courts and putting green open to public.)

though now of no importance, has figured prominently in Parliamentary records. Leland wrote, "This Bossenny hath beene a bygge thing for a fischar town," and spoke in his time of the "ruines of a gret numbre of houses". Until the Reform Act, 1832, Bossiney, in conjunction with Tintagel, returned two members to Westminster. The electors numbered twenty-five, but nine only, belonging to one family, exercised the franchise. In recent years Bossiney has become popular with those who like quiet, simple quarters in a healthy and beautiful district. There is tennis at the hotel and at Bossiney Beach good bathing may be enjoyed. Here is a natural arch known as the **Elephant Rock,** because the imaginative declare the natural pillar resembles an elephant's trunk. On

Castle Hill, in the old days, the polling was declared. Locally this is known as *Bossiney Mound*, and the story goes that the Round Table is buried under it; on Midsummer's Eve it rises from the earth and shines like silver. About half a mile southeast of Bossiney is the Celtic **Pentaly Cross.**

TINTAGEL TO BOSCASTLE

The road is fairly level except for the sharp dip at the Rocky Valley. The distance is about 3½ miles. The cliff path is much longer, for several steep and difficult corners must be negotiated, but the Rocky Valley may best be appreciated by looking up it from near its mouth. In the neighbourhood of Trevalga there is a holed rock on the cliff which is known as the *Ladies' Window.*

Beyond the Rocky Valley, on the right of the road, is *Rocky Valley Hotel* and hamlet, the former once a manor-house. Within the gate is a beehive-like structure surmounted by a cross known as *St. Piran's Well*, and close to it on the right is a chapel to the same saint (recently restored). To the right of the little chapel is an old monastery. St. Nectan's Glen and the waterfall are farther along the lane. **King Arthur's Quoit,** a stone in the hedge, is farther up the main road opposite a house called The Quoit. It is in reality a Roman milestone.

Long Island, the peculiar sharp peak of which rises to a height of 300 feet, is a conspicuous object on the coast. **Condolden Barrow,** two miles inland, rises to 1,009 feet.

Situated between Tintagel and Boscastle is **Trevalga,** a small hamlet which has kept its name unchanged since Domesday. The Church, dedicated to St. Petroc, is of interest. There are traces of Norman work in the lower masonry, and the font is Norman. Near the porch is an ancient cross, 5 feet 8 inches high. From the village, a lane leads to a curious "terrace" high on the heather-covered cliff face; a wonderful spot for meditation amid glorious scenery. Close at hand, one to the south-west, one to the north-east, are the two mighty **Willaparks** with their caves and lichened cliffs. Both are over 300 feet and both have prehistoric earthworks.

A long and steep descent leads into—

BOSCASTLE

Approaches.—By bus from Bude, or from Wadebridge (*via* Tintagel). Road Routes.—*See* pp. 6–9.

Banks.—*Barclays* and *National Westminster.* (Agencies.)

Bathing.—In place of a sandy beach and bathing huts there is an excavation in the solid rock, filled by the sea at every tide. This pool is on the south side of the harbour mouth. Swimmers generally prefer nearby Bossiney.

Buses.—To Bude (connection with the service to Bideford) and to Tintagel, Camelford and Wadebridge. In the season, coaches make excursions to all places of interest.

Car Park near Bridge and at entrance to roads leading out to Harbour. A further park inland at foot of Penally Hill (free).

Distances. — (approximate). — Tintagel Castle, 4; Camelford, 5¾; Bude, 15; Launceston, 19½; Brown Willy, 10.

Early Closing Days.—Thursday and Saturday.

Fishing.—Licences for fishing in the *Valency* river can be obtained from the Rural District Centre, Camelford.

Hotels.—*Napoleon Inn; Wellington; Tolcarne; Bottreaux Guest House.*

Licensing Hours.—10.30–2.30 and 5.30–11. Sundays 12–2, 7–10.30.

Places of Worship, with hours of Sunday services: *Parish Churches,* Forrabury 8, 11 on 1st and 3rd, 6.15. Minster, 6.15 on 1st only. *Methodist*—11 and 6.

Post Office.—9 a.m. to 6 p.m.; Bank Holidays, 9 to 10.30 a.m.

Road Routes.—*See* pp. 6–9.

Youth Hostel.—Near harbour.

Boscastle consists of a number of houses scattered on a steep hillside and along a deep, picturesque valley, down which rushes a stream. This charming old-world village is practically hidden by trees from those passing down to the harbour by the main road, which runs roughly parallel to it. For this reason, most people passing through, or who are only staying for an hour or so, miss it altogether. It is well worth exploring. It is the wonderful little haven and land-locked harbour that fascinates visitors. So land-locked is it that it is necessary to walk some distance seaward from the parking places, to catch a glimpse of the ocean. It seems as if the mighty cliffs had determined that the sea should not enter, but a narrow passage has been won, first round the base of one cliff, then round the foot of another. After this double bend, a little harbour is reached. The harbour is of very ancient origin. The outer mole was destroyed by a mine in 1941 but has since been rebuilt with granite blocks from the old Laira Bridge at Plymouth. During calm weather the entry is fairly safe, provided the ship is small and answers quickly to her helm, but during a westerly gale the haven is a cauldron of seething waves, lashing themselves against the confining rocks and then against each other, as if in savage impotence at their inability to widen the passage. But that is only one picture. Another tale is told of a setting sun throwing shafts of yellow light inside the valley against purple shadows cast by fantastic cliffs whose mighty heads seem to grow higher as the sun lowers to the sea; of blossom-laden bowers, where the scent of the honeysuckle hangs heavy in the evening air and where song-birds pour out their hearts.

Many lovers of Cornwall proudly claim that the coast scenery of Boscastle is unequalled in wild and rugged beauty and variety. From the Bridge there is a path on each side of the stream. That on the left leads to the **Bathing Pool** and **Willapark,** with its Board of Trade look-out, while at the extremity of the right-hand walk the headland which guards the entrance to the haven can be climbed. Good views of the adjacent cliffs are revealed at every turn. Note the profile rock from above the bathing-pool. The little island out at sea is **Meachard.** There is a blow-hole in the harbour—a natural hole through the narrow neck of land leading out to Penally Head. At certain states of tide, particularly with an off-sea wind, water surges through the hole with a terrific roaring noise and a jet of spray and foam is thrown across the harbour entrance. The harbour and much of the surrounding coast land is National Trust property.

Forrabury Church (St. Symphorian), on the top of the hill inland, has a worn, weather-beaten appearance. It can be reached by a footpath across Forrabury Common from Willapark. Its situation is magnificent, and it contains many features of interest, including the south porch, with roof of granite slabs, and the bench-ends in the altar table. South of the churchyard, by the road, is a fine old cross, 5 feet 7 inches high.

The Rev. R. S. Hawker wrote a dramatic poem on "The Silent Tower of Bottreaux." The church tower is minus a peal, and the poem, founded on local legend, relates how a vessel carrying some bells for this church was wrecked. The voyage was all but over, and the pilot uttered a pious "Thank God" for a safe passage. The captain, however, cried: "Thank God on land; but at sea thank the captain and the good ship." An avenging storm quickly arose; ship, captain, crew, and bells were all lost, but the pilot reached land, the only soul saved.

> "Still when the storm of Bottreaux's waves
> Is wakening in his weedy caves,
> Those bells that sullen surges hide
> Peal their deep notes beneath the tide."

Forrabury Common provides one of the few remaining survivals of "strip" or "open field" cultivation, common in Anglo-Saxon times. The strips, known locally as "stitches" and separated by low banks, are cultivated by individual farmers holding the right to them in spring and summer, but become common grazing from the end of October to the end of February.

Minster Church lies farther inland on the side of the Valency valley (*see* below). It is easily reached by car by turning to the left at a cross-way near the top of the old village, and again to the left down and then up a hill. There is also a footpath over fields from the sharp bend on the Camelford road near the top of the hill and another along the valley from near the *Cobweb Inn*. The church is beautifully situated amidst the trees, where it is almost encircled by the road which, with steep ups and downs, leads to Lesnewth. It is dedicated to St. Merthiana.

The Valency Valley

The deep combe in which Boscastle stands is watered by the rivers Valency and Jordan, affording good trout-fishing. The valley scenery is charming, one side thickly wooded, the other bare, and the playground of lights and shadows. This, the favourite inland walk from Boscastle, extends for about three miles, and is entered beyond the bridge, a signboard by "Checklands", at the foot of Penally Hill, indicating the path. If one part of the valley can be said to be more beautiful than another it is where a second cleft in the hill leads off on the right. At the head of the last-mentioned valley is **Minster Church**, in a romantic situation. A priory once existed here, of which the church formed part. **Lesnewth Valley**, another lovely spot, is a mile or so farther on. The explorer of these valleys will also want to visit **St. Juliot,** with a church containing a fine carved barrel roof and three old crosses in the graveyard.

It is of interest to admirers of Thomas Hardy, who, as a young man, was the architect in charge of the church restoration, and married, as his first wife, the rector's sister-in-law to whom, after her death, Hardy erected a memorial in the church. It can be reached by a lane from Lesnewth, which is possible for cars, though steep, with a water splash through the Valency. The lane continues up past the Church, Tremorle Farm, and on to the main road between Boscastle and Tresparrett Posts.

There is a footpath up the Valency Valley to the Church.

BOSCASTLE TO CRACKINGTON HAVEN

After mounting the high hill on the north side of the harbour, a walk of a mile leads to **Pentargon Bay,** but the cliffs all along this coast are crumbling, and although it is possible to continue along the cliff, it is advisable to approach Pentargon by way of the footpath, entered at a swing-gate on the left of the Bude road not far from Penally House. The view of the cove, with its dark perpendicular cliffs, is strangely impressive. There are caves and a fine waterfall here. *Landslides have carried away parts of the path down the cliff.* It is best to return to the main road and about a mile or less higher up take the lane on the left to Beeny, from which the cliffs can again be reached. Passing the **Beeny Sisters** out at sea, the lane climbs steeply to the stern and magnificent perpendicular **High Cliff,** 735 feet high, the highest cliff on the coast. This is a stiff walk, and many people are content to follow from Beeny the lanes and tracks which roughly follow the coast a short way inland to the farm of Trevigue. From time to time it is possible to reach the cliff either for a view seawards or to diversify the walk. The headland stretching out to sea ahead is **Cambeak,** a precipitous cliff, but the track bears more inland and leads down to the thickly wooded gorge, with a stream tumbling to the sea at the picturesque spot known as—

Crackington Haven

(6 miles from Boscastle). *See also* p. 140.

Motorists approaching from Tresparrett should note that the descent to the haven is steep (1 in 6) and winding. At the foot, the road passes across a bridge beside a car park.

The haven is at the mouth of an extremely picturesque valley, flanked by towering cliffs and thickly covered with heather, bracken and innumerable wild flowers. Within a few yaros of the shore are small hotels and guest-houses, while the district is also popular with campers. There is a small private tennis club which sometimes has vacancies for temporary members. Bathing and surfing are excellent.

From the beach a footpath leads upward to the top of Penkenna (400 feet above sea level) from which the views of rocky coastline and wooded valley are truly magnificent. The headland may also be reached by footpath from St. Gennys church and the coastal path can be followed for some miles in both directions.

A bus between Bude and Boscastle, Tintagel and Camelford (*via* Wainhouse Corner) passes through Crackington Haven on its way up to Tresparrett Posts. From Wainhouse Corner, walkers may prefer the precipitous but less frequented by-road through Rosecare hamlet. A mile above the Haven is a road at a fork which leads to **St. Gennys,** half a mile inland.

St. Gennys Church, with its sturdy low tower, finely situated on a slope high above the sea, is dedicated to St. Genesius, a martyr who is said to have carried his head after decapitation. There is a Norman tower, said to be the oldest in Cornwall, though the upper storey with its pinnacles is a restoration. The square font of Tintagel greenstone like that at Egloshayle (p. 81) is Transition-Norman. There are several interesting memorials including an ancient granite tomb in the churchyard inscribed in large embossed letters: HERE LIETH THE BODI OF BENET MIL 1593 AND THE BODI OF CHRISTOPHER BLIGH.

Much of the coast near Crackington Haven is now National Trust property. The whole area has been designated as one of outstanding natural beauty.

Bodmin

Access.—By rail, bus and coach services.

Angling.—In the Came and Fowey rivers (trout, sea trout and salmon).

Banks.—*Barclays, Lloyds, Midland, Trustee Savings.*

Bowling.—Green near the Barracks.

Car Park.—Mount Folly (in front of Assize Hall), Priory Park, Dennison Road.

Cinema.—*Palace Theatre*, Fore Street.

Distance (by road).—London, 234; Exeter, 64; Liskeard, 13; Lostwithiel, 6; Plymouth, 32; Truro, 25; Newquay, 20; Wadebridge, 7; Boscastle, 19.

Early Closing Day.—Wednesday.

Fairs.—Whitsun (pleasure fair); St. Lawrence annual fair, about October 20.

Hotels.—*Queen's Head; Westberry Hotel; Barley Sheaf Guest House; Bosvenna Guest House.*

Hunting.—North Cornwall, East Cornwall Hunts, Bolventor Harriers.

Library.—Town and district branch, Cornwall County Library, Lower Bore Street. Museum at Victoria Barracks.

Places of Worship.—*St. Petroc's* (Parish Church, 8, 11, 6.15); *Methodist* (Centenary), 11 and 6.30 ; *Roman Catholic* 8, 11 and 6.30; *Congregational* (*Lady Huntingdon's*) 6.30; *Elim and Seventh Day Adventists.*

Population.—7950.

Post Office.—St. Nicholas Street (near the Assize Hall); Sub-Office in Higher Bore Street.

Railway.—Bodmin Road on Western Region main line (3 miles: bus service).

Regimental Museum.—Victoria Barracks. Mondays to Fridays, 9–12.30 and 2–4.45. Saturdays, 9–12.30.

Road Route leaves Newquay *via* Narrowcliff Promenade, thence runs inland *via* Quintrel Downs to the Bodmin–Land's End Road, which is followed eastward past the Wireless station. Another road is *via* St. Columb Minor and Major. For other road routes, see pp. 6–9.

Bodmin, the county town, is an excellent centre from which to tour Cornwall, being only about 12 miles from north and south coasts and on the south-western fringe of Bodmin Moor, the highest points of which are Brown Willy (1,375 ft.) and Rough Tor (1,311 ft.).

The town is the headquarters of anglers using the Camel river, a very good trout and salmon stream. It was the county's principal town before the Norman Conquest and has had an interesting and often exciting history—much of it bound up with its Priory before 1539. As a religious centre it owed much to Guron, later canonized, who founded a hermitage in the valley about the year 530. Petroc, his successor, founded a monastery. He was one of the greatest figures, as Abbot and Confessor, in the Celtic Church, and died in 564. He, too, was canonised.

The burgesses are mentioned in a Pipe Roll dated 1190, but until the Dissolution the Prior was lord of the town; the early charters were granted to the Prior and not until the charter granted by Queen Elizabeth I in 1562 was Bodmin a free borough. The last important charter was granted by George III in 1798. The charters and many other Bodmin borough documents are now in the County Records Office, Truro. In 1497 Bodmin was one of the chief centres of the rebellion led by Joseph and Flamank (two Cornishmen) against a tax imposed by the King; in the same year Perkin Warbeck proclaimed himself king at Bodmin. The town also saw much of both armies in the Civil War; the Cornish Royalists had their head-quarters here for a time.

St Petroc's Church, of noble proportions, is the largest parish church in the county. It stands near where the main roads from Launceston and Liskeard enter the town. Norman work in the base of the tower shows that there was an earlier Church on the site; but the Church standing today was built between 1469 and 1471 by the townspeople, notably helped by their gilds. The fan vaulting in the porch roof is a very good specimen of medieval stone groining. The lectern, made up of parts of the old choir stalls, and the pulpit are fine examples of fifteenth-century carving. Records of the building of the Church and of the contract for the woodwork are preserved in the County Record Office, Truro. The clergy stalls and reredos, composed of original screen panels and bench-ends, were reset in their present position to the design of Sir Charles Nicholson in 1932. The splendid altar tomb of Prior Vyvyan, the last Prior but one before the Dissolution, is on the north side of the sanctuary; it originally stood in front of the High Altar of the former Priory Church, of which only a few fragments of stone remain. Remains of the fifteenth-century wagon roof should be noticed in the Lady Chapel. The organ has been moved to the west end and the north aisle converted to the military chapel of St. Maurice, where are hung the colours of the Duke of Cornwall's Light Infantry. The font is an outstanding example of late Norman undercut work.

The two parvise chambers over the south porch are of unusual interest, the more so since in one of them was found the ivory casket which once contained the relics of St. Petroc. This is now to be seen in a shrine in the south wall. The casket is that in which Roger, the Prior of Bodmin, in 1177, brought back the relics of St. Petroc which a canon of the Priory had filched and taken to Brittany.

In the churchyard is the chantry chapel of St. Thomas of Canterbury, erected in 1377. It fell into disuse at the Reformation but was later used as a school. It was preserved from complete ruin in 1935.

The little stone building over **St. Guron's Well** at the west end of the churchyard and the sixteenth-century fountain beside the road near by, bear no relation to the antiquity of the well, the water from which Bodmin people have drunk from time immemorial.

The town's **Library** building was given by Passmore Edwards. The **Assize Hall** and the near-by Shire House (Judge's Lodgings) were built in 1837; the Assize Hall and neighbouring Public Rooms stand on the site of the former conventual buildings of the Friary of the Franciscan Order.

No reference to Bodmin, however slight, is complete without an allusion to the suppression of Arundell's rebellion in 1549. After the insurgent leaders had been captured, Sir Anthony Kingston, the Provost-Marshal, wrote to Nicholas Boyer, Mayor of Bodmin, announcing his intention of dining with him, and the latter made suitable preparations. Before dinner the Provost took the Mayor aside and whispered that execution must that day be done in the town, and desired that a gallows might be erected by the time dinner was ended. The Mayor complied. When dinner was over the Provost asked to be taken to the gallows, and when he saw them inquired of the Mayor if they were strong enough. "Yes," said the Mayor, "doubtless they are." "Well, then," said the Provost, "get up speedily, for they are prepared for you, for you have been a busy rebel."

The prominent granite Obelisk (144 ft. high) on **Beacon Hill** was erected in 1856 to the memory of Walter Raleigh Gilbert, Lieutenant-General in the Bengal army, who was a native of Bodmin.

In the neighbourhood are remains of several ancient earthworks, including Castle Canyke, Dunmere camp and a Roman camp at Tregear. Near Nanstallon, coins of Vespasian (A.D. 69) and Trajan (A.D. 98–117) were found as well as rings, spearheads and fragments of Roman pottery.

In addition to the Priory of St. Petroc and an establishment of Franciscan Friars there were formerly several ancient chapels in the neighbourhood: St. Leonard, St. Nicholas, St. Anthony, St. George, St. Ann, St. Margaret, and the Lazar Hospital of St. Lawrence, all of which lend their names to parts of the town and district. While so rich in historical associations Bodmin is also the centre of much fine and varied scenery, from the wild, rolling hills of the moor to the beauties of the Glynn and Camel valleys.

There are several ancient crosses near Bodmin.

Dunmere Woods, with the Camel river running through, are of great beauty, and the visitor who finds himself in Bodmin with a few hours to spare should pay a visit to the village of **Cardynham** (4 miles).

Walkers leave Bodmin by the road past the church, turning to the right along the Liskeard road, and half a mile farther along taking the Turfdown-Fletchersbridge turning to the left. At Turfdown a lane leads on the left to the banks of a stream. Here is the entrance to a State Forest and the entry of cars is prohibited, but walkers may make their way through the glen till they arrive at a farm gate leading out to Milltown, near Cardynham.

On a hill stands *St. Meubred*, Cardynham, a fine old Cornish church principally in the style of the fifteenth century. In the church-yard are two important ancient crosses, one of which opposite the south door ranks among the finest Celtic crosses in England. Inside the church should be noted the fine carved roofs of the aisles; the Transition-Norman font; the carved bench-ends; Charles I's Letter of Thanks; and good modern windows at the east end.

Motorists can take one of two routes: (*a*) Go to Turfdown as described above, then on to Fletchersbridge, and by a narrow, steep road with fine views emerge at Cardynham Church, with the earth-works of Cardynham Castle on the right. (*b*) From Bodmin take the left-hand (Launceston) road, A30, which, passing over the Race-course Downs, has magnificent open views. At Four Winds, 3½ miles, turn to the right, and at Treslea, or "Bargain Cross", 2 miles, sharply to the right again, reaching Cardynham Church in about half a mile. It makes an interesting round to go one way and return the other.

A few miles south-west of Bodmin is a Beam Wireless Station.

Two and a half miles south-east of Bodmin is **Lanhydrock,** the seat of the Robartes family, prominent in Cornish history. The church contains several monuments, and there is a fine cross, 8 feet in height. Lanhydrock House, a mansion of the late Jacobean period, has a remarkable Long Gallery. The battlemented barbican is conspicuous. The House and Gardens are held by the National Trust. Open from April to mid-October daily except Sundays and Mondays (open Bank Holidays), *charge.*

Blisland (*Royal Oak Inn*) is reached by car from Bodmin by a turn to the left 3½ miles along the Launceston road. If continuing the round from Cardynham, go straight on at the Four Winds crossing and at Whitecross, 1 mile, take the right-hand road which soon descends steeply to a narrow picturesque bridge and then rises to the church which faces the village from the other side of the green.

The village, one of the most picturesque in Cornwall, has a green (the only one in the County) shaded by many fine ash and sycamore trees. An ancient sheep fair is held each year, generally the last Monday of September.

Blisland Church, dedicated to SS. Protus and Hyacinth, is quite unlike most Cornish churches, which are as a rule rather sombre. It has a brilliantly coloured Rood Screen of intricate design and a fine wagon roof.

On the north-eastern boundary of the parish Bradford and Delford bridges over the De Lank stream are good examples of Cornish stone bridges.

On the main Bodmin–Launceston road is **Temple,** where was once a chapel of the Knights-Templars of Jerusalem. Here, according to Hals, by ancient right the vicar or curate could legally marry all persons, man and woman, that "applye to them without banns or license". After the dissolution of the Order in 1312 the church gradually fell into ruin. It was eventually rebuilt in 1883. The Norman font remains. The ancient base of this font, discovered too late to be of use, is built into the inner wall of the church over the doorway. Many curious grave-stones and crosses which came to light during excavations have been incorporated into the wall of an outbuilding.

Another excursion easily made from Bodmin is that to **Dozmary Pool** (*see* p. 89), with its Arthurian and other legends.

Launceston

Angling.—There is good angling on the Tamar, the Inney and other streams of the neighbourhood.

Banks.—*Barclays, Lloyds, Midland; National Westminster*, Westgate Street; *Savings Bank*, Exeter Street.

Bowls.—Two clubs—Kensey Vale and Dunheved.

Buses.—To Tavistock and Plymouth, to Wadebridge and Newquay *via* Camelford, to Bideford and Bude. Royal Blue coach services to West Cornwall, Exeter and London.

Car Parks.—Main car park at the market. Also at Town Hall and in the Square.

Cinema.

Distances.—Bodmin, 22; Camelford, 17; Bude, 19; Boscastle, 19; Plymouth, 27.

Early Closing.—Thursday.

Excursions.—Coach trips to most places of interest in Cornwall and on the Devon border.

Golf.—St. Stephens, 18 holes. Putting Green, Coronation Park.

Hotels.—*White Hart*, The Square; *Eagle*

House, Castle Street.

Hunting.—With the Lamerton, Tetcott or East Cornwall Foxhounds.

Licensing Hours.—11–2.30 and 5–10.30, Sundays, 12–2, 7–10.30.

Market Days.—Saturday (Pannier) Tuesday (Cattle).

Museum.—Lawrence House, in Castle Street.

Places of Worship.—*St. Mary Magdalene*, 8, 11, 6.30; *St. Stephen*, 8, 10, 6 or 7; *St. Thomas*, 11, 6 or 7; *Methodist, Roman Catholic.*

Population.—4,700.

Post Office.—Westgate Street, 9.00 a.m. to 5.30 p.m.

Road Route from Newquay *via* Bodmin. Go right through Bodmin, turning to left at the foot of Bore Street, then bearing to right, past church, and ascending sharply to the open road across the moors to Launceston (about 42 miles from Newquay).

Tennis.—At Coronation Park. (Swimming Pool.)

No one approaching Launceston (pronounced Launston) from the north can fail to appreciate its importance in early days, for it crowns a hill that rises almost perpendicularly from the valley of the little *Kensey* river—an inevitable site for a castle.

Often described as "The Gateway to Cornwall"—owing to its position just across the border from Devon—the town stands high above its immediate surroundings, in the centre of some of the finest moorland scenery in the west of England.

Launceston (ancient capital of the Duchy), is a venerable place, with the indefinable atmosphere of a cathedral city. It is the *Lauscavetone* of Domesday, and is sometimes known by its Norman title of *Dunheved* meaning "a city on a hill." Dunheved was incorporated as a free borough by Richard, Earl of Cornwall, and the borough had a mayor as early as 1257. In 1259 it returned two members to Parliament.

The town has much to interest those who take a pride in

110

historicaı buildings, churches, bridges and gateways; quaint alleys, flagged courtyards, peaceful old squares and terraces. In contrast to these picturesque features are many excellent modern shops, together with a number of hotels and guest-houses and modern industrial sites at Scarne and Pennygillam. Launceston has a **Regional Library,** an interesting **Museum** in Lawrence House, Castle Street, and a modern, well-patronised **Swimming Bath.** There are also **Constitutional** and **Liberal Clubs, Ex-Service Club, North Cornwall Motor Club,** among others, **Cinema, Recreation Grounds, Park,** and ample facilities for all kinds of sport. In the **Guildhall** are some old paintings, and the insignia of the Corporation are interesting. The borough seal dates from 1573. A wealth of royal charters is contained in the Borough Archives.

The centre of the town is **The Square,** used as a short period **Car Park.** Here is the War Memorial, an excellent reproduction of an old market cross.

The chief attraction to visitors is—

Launceston Castle

Open, March, April, Weekdays, 9.30–5.30, Sundays, 2–5.30; May–Sept., 9. 30–7 2–7; Nov.–Feb., 10–4.30, 2–4.30.

This is a grand old ruin com-manding splendid views and surrounded by pleasant grounds and is only a few minutes' walk from the centre of the town. From the War Memorial go to the west end of the Square, and turn down to the right for 150 yards. There is no charge for admission to the Castle Green but the Keep is now in the care of the Ministry of Public Building and Works and a small charge is made.

The approach to the Keep from the grounds is up a long flight of stone steps. The view from the doorways and pathways surround-ing the Keep is astonishing. The climb up to the town seems onerous enough, yet from the

111

Castle we look down at it from quite a dizzy height. The wide view is particularly impressive to the west, where the heights of Bodmin Moor, Brown Willy and Rough Tor break against the skyline. The north gate, which is not within the fenced-off portion, is the best-preserved part, with a room on one side. A notice states that George Fox, founder of the Society of Friends, was, with other Quakers, immured here ("in Doomsdale") for eight months in 1656, for distributing religious papers in West Cornwall.

Ancient writers differ as to when and by whom "Castle Terrible" was built. The opinion of the Launceston Scientific and Historical Society, after careful research, is that the Castle was begun about the time of Edward the Confessor, who strengthened or pulled down and rebuilt so many Saxon strongholds. The original castle was probably of timber. Much of the masonry structure belongs to the first half of the thirteenth century and may be due to Richard, Earl of Cornwall. William I gave the Castle to his half-brother, the Earl of Mortain. It reverted to Edward III, who bestowed it on Edward the Black Prince, first Duke of Cornwall. It is interesting to observe that, although during the Civil Wars it had various temporary ownerships, the sequence of inheritance by the Dukes of Cornwall and Princes of Wales, heirs to the British Crown, has survived to the present day.

At the outbreak of the Civil War, Sir Richard Bullen held Launceston Castle for the Parliament, but was quickly dispossessed by Sir Ralph Hopton and his army, three thousand strong. He was assisted by that doughty warrior, Sir Bevill Grenville, and together they repulsed an attack by Major-General Sir George Chudleigh, who did yeoman service for the Parliament in North Devon. The Castle capitulated to Cromwell's forces in the following year, 1644, but quickly reverted to the Royalists, as the Parliamentary campaign in Cornwall was not then very vigorously pursued. The Prince of Wales, afterwards Charles II, stopped at the Castle a short while in the course of his flight westward. In 1645 the Castle had for its defender a notable figure, Sir Richard Grenville, followed by Colonel Basset. Early in the next year Sir Thomas Fairfax renewed hostilities, and a vigorous campaign in the West soon led to the submission of Devon and Cornwall to the Parliament. Launceston Castle surrendered in 1646.

Since that period until taken over by the Ministry of Works in 1951, the Castle has been in the nominal charge of Constables. The latter-day wardens—Mayors of Launceston—have been more mindful of their duties than were their predecessors, who took no care to preserve the stronghold.

In their capacity as Dukes of Cornwall, King George V and the Duke of Windsor visited the Castle in 1909 and 1921 respectively—in both cases when Prince of Wales. King George VI, however, was already crowned when in 1937 he made a state entry into the Castle, being welcomed with age-old ceremonial and presented with feudal dues—a pound of pepper and one hundred shillings, which were set down in a charter of 1230 by Richard, King of the Romans, then Earl of Cornwall.

Elephant Rock, Bossiney Cove

Trebarwith Strand

The Cliffs, near Tintagel

Launceston Priory

When the North Cornwall Railway was being constructed in 1886, the remains of the priory were discovered in an adjoining meadow, close to the present gasworks. The spot is approached by a doorway in St. Thomas's churchyard; from the castle go down Northgate Street to the River Kensey and then along it as far as a beautiful old stone foot-bridge—the Prior's Bridge.

It was here that the "Waterfeire" was held in ancient times, and witches ducked. Some of the remains first discovered were carefully preserved in the Museum. Further excavations followed until the original plan of all the buildings was discovered. To prevent encroachment by modern buildings, the field was bought by local subscription and enclosed by the Launceston Antiquarian Society. They are now the property of the local town council. Only portions have been laid bare and notices state what they represent. The foundations unearthed are supposed to have been laid about 1126. The Priory was completed in 1140 when the Augustinians, installed by Bishop Warelwast of Exeter in the reign of Henry I, moved from St. Stephens. It is evident that the buildings were very extensive. The Norman doorway at the *White Hart Hotel* was part of this ancient Priory. Other portions of the Priory were incorporated in St. Thomas's Church; some have been used in adjacent houses. The Priory, in fact, was regarded as a quarry, and the civic records show items for "drawing stone from the Priory".

St. Thomas's Church, though not as ornate as St. Mary's, described below, has many features of interest, including a very beautiful square font, probably brought from the Priory, fine pillars and arches, and good linen-fold panelling. The church appears to have been connected officially with the Castle, for felons were buried in the churchyard, and there were many references to judicial proceedings in the church accounts.

St. Mary Magdalene Church,

consecrated in 1524, is a remarkable building. There is scarcely a square foot of its exterior walls that is not decorated with quatrefoils, shields, fleurs-de-lis, Latin inscriptions, coats-of-arms, saints, foliage, and other devices rather coarsely executed. The whole is worth careful study, for there is not another church in the county like it.

From the chancel door eastward round the building is a Latin inscription, beginning "Ave Maria". The fine porch has an upper

chamber. In front are the weather-worn arms of Trecarrell and Kelway and the date 1511. The tower is fourteenth-century. The church has some notable woodwork, new and old; note the screen, the roof, the pulpit, and the bench-ends. The font is old, though re-tooled. There are many interesting memorials.

On the north side of the church-yard note on a tombstone the ancient cross head. The shaft is modern.

St. Stephen's Church stands on the summit of the hill north of Launceston, at the end of the part called **Newport** as distinct from **Dunheved** south of the river. A Collegiate Church has stood here since before the Conquest and is mentioned in the Domesday Book. When the monastery was moved in 1140 to Kenseyvale the Church became a parish Church. It was rebuilt in 1259 and enlarged in 1419. It has a high tower, fine studded door and magnificent round font with vine and cable design. There are two interesting Romanesque stone carvings on the east wall.

On the way up to St. Stephen's is the **Roman Catholic Church** dedicated to the English Martyrs.

The Early English **South Gate** of the town, a fine structure, remains. The rooms in the upper storey were once used as the town "lock-up".

The **Windmill**, a fine open space for rest and recreation, approached from the Square by way of Westgate Street and a steep hill, stands 585 feet above sea-level and commands magnificent views in all directions. Below the Windmill is the Coronation Park with swimming baths and tennis courts.

In the neighbourhood of Launceston are many beautiful villages, churches and crosses, some of which are passed on the main roads, but the most interesting are only to be found by following cross-country roads and lanes, some of them rustic and half-hidden. A lovely drive is from Launceston along the Bodmin road (A30) turning right at Five Lanes to **Altarnun** (*see* below). Cross the bridge and after a mile turn left. Two hundred yards farther turn right, and in another mile sharply right again by an inn. A further right turn leads in a little more than a mile down to the river Inny and up to **St. Clether** (*see* below). Continuing past St. Clether the narrow road, which has cattle grids, emerges onto the Launceston–Camelford road (A395). This picturesque but devious route is necessary owing to the slope of the valley and the marshy nature of the ground. For walkers there are several more direct footpaths.

The name **Altarnun** means "The Altar of St. Nonna", a Welsh saint, patron also of a parish in Brittany. There is a beautiful cross in the churchyard, and the Norman font, fifteenth-century high tower, fifteenth-century carved wagon roofs and rood screen are striking features. The greatest treasures of the church, however, are the magnificent solid bench-ends. They are 79 in number and are most richly carved with the Instruments of the Passion, a man with a cauldron, a man playing bagpipes, a fiddler, etc.

Four miles farther south-west along the Bodmin road from Five Lanes is the village of **Bolventor** in an area of rolling hills and valleys. Its little bell-turreted church is well-seen from the A30 road. Nearby is the Jamaica Inn made famous by Daphne du Maurier.

St. Clether, 9 miles west of Launceston, and 2 miles north-west of Altarnun, is notable for a beautiful example of the little wayside chapels which were numerous in pre-Norman times. Nearly all of them were destroyed at the Reformation, but this one, built in the fifteenth century on the site of an earlier one, was spared, although it became ruined. It was beautifully restored by the late Rev. S. Baring-Gould, and fortunately its most interesting feature remains as it was in the past; that is, the little stream which flows from the beautiful Holy Well into the chapel, passing behind the stone altar, and out through a recess in the opposite wall into a second well. (The key of the chapel may be found in the porch).

St. Clether's Church, from which the chapel may be reached by crossing the beautiful glebe fields sloping down to the river, was built in 1225 and dedicated some years later by Bishop Bronescombe of Exeter. It suffered drastic restoration in the nineteenth century, but a Saxon font, Norman pillars with scalloped capitals and late medieval tower remain. Standing almost alone, except for the vicarage, it has a lovely woodland setting and serves a small scattered population.

On the other side of the valley is the Manor of **Basil Barton,** one of the finest Elizabethan houses in the county. On the estate there are five round-headed crosses, which appear to have been guide stones marking tracks that led to St. Clether Well.

Bude

General Information

Access.—Bude is 219 miles by road from London. For road routes, see pp. 6–9. By rail the journey is via Exeter to Okehampton, where connection is made with Bude by coach services (26 miles).

Banks.—*Barclays; Lloyds; National Westminster*, all in Strand or Belle Vue.

Bathing.—From the beach at the foot of the sand-hills under Summerleaze Downs, Crooklets, and at Maer Lake Cove, at the north end of the town. Huts may be hired. The tide goes a long way out and bathing from the sands at *low water* or on an ebb tide needs extreme caution. Beach patrols are in attendance. The fine breakers provide marvellous surf-bathing. Boards may be hired or purchased locally.

The excellent and extensive Bathing Pool, and the smaller and more primitive Sir Thomas' Pit, among the rocks at the end of the Breakwater, make it possible to bathe in safety and comfort at all times.

Boating.—There is practically no open-sea boating, but a pleasant little trip may be made on the Canal or on the Neet.

Bowls.—There is a fine Cumberland Turf Green at the Bude Haven Recreation Ground available to visitors.

Buses.—To Boscastle and Camelford; to Bideford (*via* Kilkhampton, Hartland and Clovelly); to Holsworthy and Torrington, etc.; to Poughill, Marhamchurch and Widemouth; to Launceston and Plymouth; to Wadebridge and Newquay and other parts. For particulars, see time-tables and bills.

Camping.—Several licensed sites within the district.

Car Parks.—Crooklets, on the northern side of the bay; The Wharf, between Shalder Hills and the Castle; Summerleaze.

Cinema.—The Picture House, Summerleaze Down. Tel.: Bude 2016.

Climate.—Fresh and bracing in summer, mild in winter. See also p. 15.

Coaches make regular trips in the season to Clovelly, Boscastle and Tintagel, Hartland, Bideford, Westward Ho!. Morwenstow, Lydford Gorge and other favourite resorts.

Cricket.—On Summerleaze Down.

116

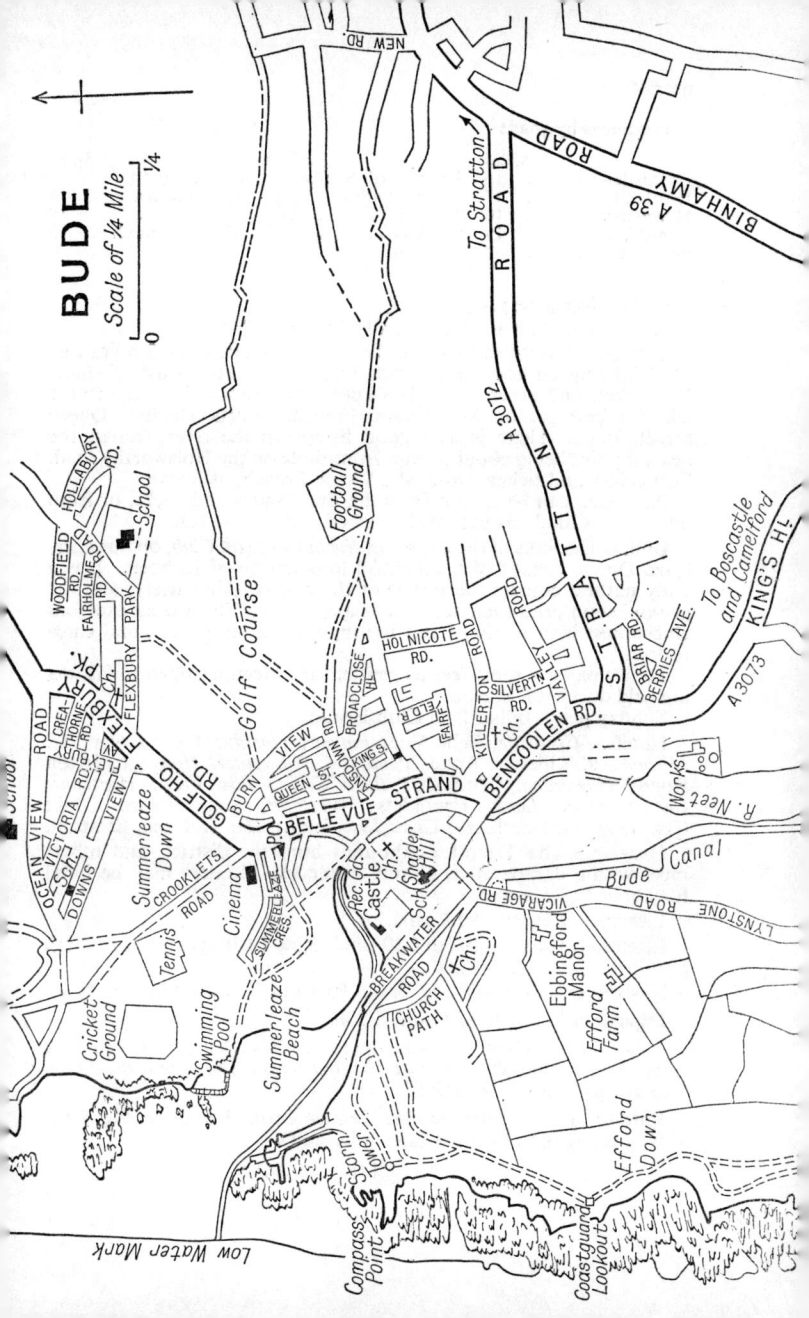

Distances by road:

	Miles		Miles		Miles
Boscastle	16	Widemouth Sands	2	Kilkhampton	6
Hartland	17	Combe Valley	5	Morwenstow	8
Holsworthy	10	Tintagel	20	Launceston	19
Camelford	19	Clovelly	16½	Marhamchurch	2
Poughill	2	Stratton	2		

Early Closing Day.—Thursday.

Fair.—Bude Fair is held annually on Sept. 22nd.

Fishing.—Trout-fishing in the Tamar Reservoir, some 2 miles east of Kilkhampton and, in a direct line, 6 miles north-east of Bude. For tickets and other particulars application should be made to the lakeside cottage, or Mr. Victor French, Sports Dealer, Queen Street, Bude. There is also good fishing in the river Tamar, the nearest point being about 5 miles from Bude on the Holsworthy road. Particulars and tickets from Mr. Victor French, as above.

Bass, etc., can be caught from the Breakwater and rocks, or from boats; the Canal has been well stocked with coarse fish.

Golf.—The links of the *Bude and North Cornwall Club*, on Summerleaze Down, consist of a delightful long course of 18 holes. It is a truly natural course; the turf is of the real seaside variety, and the ground soon dries even after the heaviest rain. There is an excellent club-house with reading- and writing-rooms, tea-rooms, and card-rooms.

Ladies pay the same fees as gentlemen. Meetings open to visitors are held during the season.

Sunday play. Billiards in Club House.

Hotels.—*Grenville*. Belle Vue; *Falcon; Florida; Maer Lodge; St. Margaret's*, Killerton Road; *Penarvor; Penwethers House*, Killerton Road; *Hawarden*, Crooklets; *Burn Court; Bay View; Hartland; Ceres; Maer Lake*, Crooklets; *Westcliff*, Summerleaze Cres.; *Grosvenor*, Summerleaze; *Choughs*, Upton; *The Tree Inn*, Stratton.

Hunting.—The Tetcott Foxhounds hunt the district, and others meet within comparatively short distances. Hunters may be hired for about £2 2s. a day.

Library.—County, the Castle.

Licensing Hours.—10.30–2.30 and 5.30–10.30 (11 in summer). Sundays, 12–2 and 7–10.30.

Newspapers.—*Cornish and Devon Post* and *Western Morning News*.

Population.—(Bude-Stratton) 5,200.

Post Office.—Head Office at the top of Belle Vue, 8.30 a.m.–5.30 p.m. There are sub-offices at Flexbury and The Crescent, Bude, and at Stratton and Poughill.

Putting, at the Summerleaze Tennis Ground and on the Bude Haven Recreation Ground (also mini-golf).

118

Places of Worship, with hours of Sunday services:

St. Michael's (Parish Ch.)—H.C. 8; Sung Eucharist and Sermon, 10; Matins and Sermon, 11.15; Evensong, 6.

Congregational—St. Martins, Killerton Road, 11 and 6.

Methodist (near Nanny Moore's Bridge and at Flexbury Park)—11 a.m. and 8 p.m. (summer) 6 p.m. (winter).

Catholic—Church of St. Peter, Sundays—Mass, 8 a.m. and 10.30 a.m. Evening service 6 p.m.

Many visitors walk out to the fine old churches at Stratton and Poughill. There is a pleasant footpath to the former, much more attractive than the road (*see* p. 125).

Recreation Ground.—Bude Haven, nine hard tennis courts, squash court, bowling and putting greens. All facilities open to visitors. Weekly, monthly and season tickets may be obtained from groundsmen.

Riding.—There are several establishments from which hacks may be hired and which specialise in teaching children.

Tennis.—Twelve grass courts on Summerleaze Downs. Fortnightly tickets are issued in May, June and July. There are tennis courts on the Sports Ground at Stratton.

BUDE

Bude is laid out on the southern slopes of a broad tongue of rising land almost filling a mile-wide gap in the rocky wall that Cornwall presents to the Atlantic. There is no formal front at Bude; the "Parade" is a broad stretch of open turf bounded on the west and south by low cliffs below which are wonderful expanses of firm golden sand. If one part of the town more than another resembles a promenade it is the **Strand,** part of the business thoroughfare, bounded on one side by shops, hotels and banks, and on the other by the picturesque *Neet River,* which after considerable windings contrives here to pour its waters into the sea. The river is crossed by two bridges, either of which leads to another pleasant waterway that is recognizable as a canal only by its straightness in this last reach to the sea. Here are the *Falcon Hotel,* the parish church and some very attractively placed houses. Behind them the ground rises to resume the Cornish cliff wall; half a mile away to the north, where the ground rises again to form the magnificent cliffs on towards Hartland, is the area known as **Flexbury.**

119

Some attempt has been made to describe the peculiarly open situation of Bude, since because of its very spaciousness no photograph can do justice to the place as a whole. Although a busy little town, it is almost surrounded by open downland; and though a seaside resort it overlooks two fresh-water channels. That it is an outdoor resort should need no emphasising. Bathing and surfing, tennis, golf, bowls, cricket, rowing, riding, hunting—practically every sport is followed with zest, and the wide grass-covered expanse, known as **Summerleaze Downs,** with the glorious sands, render it an ideal playground for children. Moreover, when the winds are too boisterous to make the sands or the downs altogether pleasant, there are many sheltered combes and villages easily accessible a mile or so inland. As a centre for the exploration of the country between the Camel and the Torridge, Bude is unrivalled.

The district possesses an equable climate. Frost and snow are rare, and the summer heat is tempered by the Atlantic breezes. The records show that Bude enjoys an exceptional number of hours of bright sunshine.

The town is, like most young resorts, somewhat uneven, but there are good shops, and well-lighted streets. There is an excellent supply of pure water and the drainage is thoroughly efficient. The reservoirs, 2 miles east of Kilkhampton, are stocked with fish (*see* p. 118).

Modern terraces, with most of the houses catering for guests, extend in all directions, but sheltered by the adjacent downs. The broad **Strand** runs beside the river towards the business part of the town, continued by **Belle Vue,** near the top of which is the **Post Office,** beyond which, on the top of Summerleaze

Down is the **Cinema.** A turning up to the right, at the foot of Belle Vue, leads to the **Parish Hall,** used for concerts, etc.

Opposite the Strand and across the river is a large tract of land, which the Canal on

BUDE AND DISTRICT

English Miles

0   1   2   3

WARD, LOCK & CO. LIMITED, LONDON

© John Bartholomew & Son Ltd, Edinburgh

Gull Rock
Marsland
Yeol Mouth
Cornakey
Cory
Henna Cliff
Bryaton
Morwenstow
Inn Crosstown
Rusmoor
Higher Sharpnose Pt.
Tidnacoombe
Stanbury
Darste
Ham
Woodford
Hippa Rock
Stanburymouth
Harscott
Lower Sharpnose Pt.
Cleave
Woodla
N.T.
Coombe
Burridge
Steeple Pt.
Camp
Warren Pt.
Stowe Barton
Warren Gutter
Houndapit
Stibb
Sandy Mouth
Scadghill
Long Rock
Tiscott
Menachurch Pt.
Northcott
Northcott Mouth
Maer Cliff
Maer
Ponghill
B U D E
Flexbury Park
Summerleaze
Wrangle Pt.
Bude Haven
BUDE
Compass Pt.
Efford Beacon
King's Hill
Bagbury
B A Y
Lynstom
Thorne
Upton Roddsbridge
Phillips's Point
Whalesborough
Higher Longbeak
Helebridge
Lower Longbeak
Salthouse
Hilscott
Widemouth Sand
Creathorne
Moor
Woolston
Widemouth Villa
Langford
Wanson Mouth
Widemouth
Foxhole Pt.
Wanson
Wheellaton
Millook Haven
Penhalt
Burracott
Coppathorne
Cancleave Strand
Millook
Trevisick
Causwell
Dizzard Pt.
Poundstock
Chipman Strand
Bangors
Dyneoth Cliff
Trevolter
Treslannick
Cleave Strand
Dizzard
Trengayor
Longland
Penlean
Hele
Tresmorn
Whitenook
Trewint
Kerley
Pencannow Pt.
Cleave
St Gennys
Basard
Dimma
Dinnecoombe
Crackington Haven
Coxford
Crannow
Trenkreek
Treforda
Sudcott
Cambeak
Tremayna
Trelay
Tretida
Ash
Flanders
Rosecare
Jacobstow
Landhillick
Hallagather
Wainhouse Corner
Southcott

the farther side almost makes an island, broken by a high tussocky mound known as the **Shalder Hill.** On top, in a conspicuous position, is the **War Memorial,** overlooking the **Central Methodist Church,** and the **Drill Hall,** and on the flat ground seaward is the **Recreation Ground,** with tennis courts and bowling and putting greens and a pavilion in which table tennis and squash racquets are played. At the seaward end of this tract, sheltered by huge grassy banks, stands the **Castle** (municipal offices), built by Sir Goldsworthy Gurney, the Cornish engineer, inventor of the steam blow-pipe and of one of the earliest steam road-locomotives.

On the farther (southward) side of the Canal is the **Church of St. Michael and All Angels,** consecrated in 1835, with baptistery and font added at a later date. The vicarage in Falcon Terrace is a quaint house, known formerly as "Squint" from the fact that there is no right angle in any room. The former vicarage, Ebbingford Manor, once a manor of Sir John Arundell, of Trerice, dates from the fifteenth century, and was the gift of Sir Thos. Acland. Readers of Baring-Gould's *Hawker of Morwenstow* will remember that it was here that young Hawker at the age of nineteen proposed to Miss Charlotte I'Ans, twenty-two years his senior. At Bude, too, he deceived the people into believing that a mermaid sat, each moonlit night, on the rocks, flashing a mirror and singing mystic songs. For several nights the hoax was continued and the gathering crowds became more numerous; then young Hawker decided that it was too cold to sit on the rocks at midnight, clad only in seaweed, and thenceforward the mermaid of Bude was seen no more.

The river is spanned by two bridges, one a modern concrete structure on the Stratton road, the other an ancient device of stone and wood, known as **Nanny Moore's Bridge.** A mill stood here of old, and it is suggested that the wooden span at the western end of the bridge marks the place occupied by the wheel. Probably this was the mill whose "causey," in the words of Carew, "serveth as a verie convenient bridge, to save the way-farers former trouble, let, and daunger."

The **Bude and Holsworthy Canal** was constructed in 1819–26, at a cost of £128,000. Originally extending over 30 miles, it is now navigable for only a mile and a half, having been superseded by the railway. The Canal communicates with the sea by means of a lock, the gates of which serve as a footbridge for those who wish to ascend Compass Hill and the Downs.

Bude Haven is a small bay opening to the sea at the mouth of the river. The sand here is of darker colour than usual and is highly valued for agricultural purposes.

Bathing in the open sea at Bude is safe except at low water when it is best to use the excellent **Bathing Pool,** at the foot of the cliffs under Summerleaze Downs. The pool is one acre in extent, with graduated depths and changing tents. With its background of rocks and its views over the sands and down the coast the Pool is delightfully situated, and provides a pleasant alternative to the open sea.

In addition to this, and popular with children, is **Sir Thomas's Pit,** a small semi-natural Bathing Pool constructed by Sir Thomas Acland in the rocks near Chapel Rock, varying in depth from 2 to 6 feet.

At spring tides the water rises at Bude no less than 23 feet, at neap 17 feet, which is higher than at any other place in Cornwall. As may be imagined, with a strong wind the sea at a spring flood is a marvellous sight. The rough seas at Bude must be seen to be realised; no words can adequately describe them. Here can be seen waves mountains high, and the roar, as they break and pound the foreshore, can be heard for miles inland.

The Breakwater, reached by a path at the end of Breakwater Road, close to the lock gates, protects the Canal entrance and also serves as a promenade. Its irregular stones are certainly unconventional, but the structure affords a means of getting into close contact with the sea, and is a sheltered spot for writing or reading.

The rock with flagstaff at the end of the Breakwater is called **Chapel Rock,** from a chapel once standing here. The flagstaff was erected to assist the passage of vessels in and out of the little harbour, though there is practically no shipping at Bude these days.

The extensive **Sands** are firm and dry at low water, and are among the finest on the coast.

The cliffs which form the "front" of Bude, but actually divide the foreshore into two separate beaches, attract attention from below because of the distinctive markings and colourings of

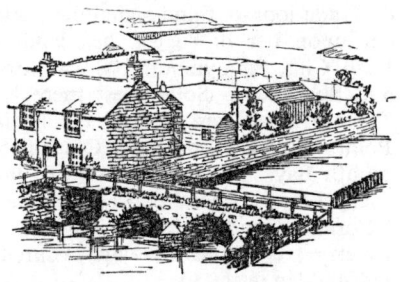

the strata. Close to the Breakwater there will be noticed peculiar contortions of rock, caused by earth movements in ancient times, and the curious **Whale Back Rock,** a long ridge broken away at one end, somewhat resembling the mounds in which farmers keep swedes through the winter.

The fine expanse of grassland separating the two parts of the town is called—

Summerleaze

Here are the **Golf Links** (*see* p. 118) of the *Bude and North Cornwall Golf Club*—but not so close to the sea as to prevent the public enjoying the cliffs to the full; in fact, the course was altered and more land acquired in order to leave the downs near the sea free and open. The views in all directions are delightful, and the invigorating sea-breezes add to the pleasure of the game.

Tennis courts and a cricket ground adjoin the golf course.

The grassy slopes on the south and west sides of Summerleaze with seats and shelter, and a café below, form a pleasant promenade.

On the Breakwater side of the Haven, a few steps lead up to a gate giving access to the path to the Breakwater and—

Compass Point,

from which a magnificent view is obtained, On the summit is an octagonal storm tower, each of its sides facing a main point of the compass. Numerous seats, offering a variety of views, are dotted about.

Southward to Widemouth extend the delightful **Efford Downs. Efford Beacon** is the highest point. Here is the Board of Trade look-out and signalling station. Looking northward, tier upon tier of rugged headlands come into sight: Maer High Cliff, Sandymouth, Morwenstow Look-out, Hennacliff and Sharpnose. South-west there is an even grander view. Trevose Head lies low on the horizon, then come Pentire Point, Tintagel, Boscastle, Crackington, Millook and Widemouth Bay. Twenty-five miles to northward looms Lundy's rocky island. Inland can be seen the Dartmoor tors and the "Cornish Giants", Rough Tor and Brown Willy, and in between a sea of hills and dales, church towers and white farms half-hidden in the trees.

Cliff Walks

Along the cliffs there are delightful walks, long or short as fancy dictates, the return being varied by using one of the inland roads. South of Efford Beacon is the impressive **Efford Ditch**, where a deep indentation has been eaten in the cliffs. After this the cliffs rise and fall alternately until the road to Widemouth is struck near a settlement of bungalows. From here the return can be made by road direct to the town near the Falcon Hotel, or by going inland past Upton by a more circuitous route across the Canal at Roddsbridge or along the towpath.

Northward of Bude the houses at Crooklets almost touch the cliff edge, so for a coast walk the path must be reached by way of the road a little way inland, turning down to the coast behind the houses or taking the rough track straight ahead. In about a mile a descent is made to **Northcott Mouth,** where is a tea-house and a road coming down from Poughill. The way is continued across the bridge by a farm track; when it turns inland at the top go out to the cliffs, passing the butts of the former rifle range; onwards is a hilly walk to **Sandymouth,** where a road leads upward to Stibb, and so back to Bude by Poughill or Stratton, a long round. The energetic may continue to **Duckpool,** at the seaward end of the charming **Combe Valley,** but all unaccustomed to rough cliff walking should remember that unexpected obstacles may appear in the way, and that it is not always possible to turn inland at inclination. Distances may actually be comparatively short, but undulations and rough going make them longer, while in wet weather miry patches and swollen streams render wide detours necessary. Picnic parties can easily reach these favourite porths by car, for all are within a short distance of the regular inland roads.

Excursions from Bude

For buses *see* p. 116. **Road Routes.** *See* pp. 6–9.

Bude is fortunately placed about midway between Clovelly, one of the most picturesque villages in the country, and Boscastle and Tintagel, the finest examples of romantic coast scenery in Cornwall. Then, too, it is a convenient centre for tours to the beautiful wooded country inland, where charming villages are linked by lovely lanes, and ancient churches stand embowered in trees. A great many excursions may be enjoyed either on foot, by car or coach. The bus services are efficient and fairly frequent.

I. TO STRATTON

Road Route.—The road to Stratton turns to the left opposite the old Station. On approaching town, take *second* turning on left.

Footpath Route.—Turn up by the *Carriers' Inn*, in the Strand, passing the power station and County school, to the edge of the golf links, where, bearing right, follow the telegraph wires. On emerging into the high-road near Stratton, walkers turn to the right and descend to the town by the old road.

Stratton is about 2 miles from Bude by road, or 1½ by the field paths off the Strand. It is a quiet little town of great antiquity and mentioned in Domesday. It was possibly a Roman station; in the Middle Ages it had a thriving industry from the salt pits.

United with Bude for purposes of local government, Stratton is set in a hollow between lofty hills, from which glorious views are gained, and it presents a charming picture when seen from the bridge over the little river Neet.

Apart from many lovely old houses, a feature of Stratton is the finely placed fourteenth-century **Church** (8, 10.30, 6 p.m.).

It contains some good examples of Norman work, some fine carvings and a timber roof. It is dedicated to St. Andrew, but Bishop Lacy's register 1430, gives St. Cristina. Here is the tomb of *Sir*

125

John Arundell (1561), with brasses showing also his two wives, seven daughters, and three sons. Sir John was Vice-Admiral of the West to Henry VIII and was knighted at the Battle of the Spurs. Note the Norman font and the curious poor-box, dated 1707, on the belfry steps. The pulpit is Jacobean, but has been restored. On a window-sill in the north aisle will be seen the old stocks, and on another sill a damaged effigy of a knight. This is supposed to represent Sir Ranulph de Blanchminster, lord of the manor in the fourteenth century. The church has been carefully restored, and a fine screen added. There are numerous interesting epitaphs in the churchyard. A modern wooden Calvary of unusual design stands outside the south porch, which bears a sundial.

Across the road, by the Post Office, there is a passage with ancient arches, and many old buildings are to be seen in the little town.

The *Tree Inn*, an ancient hostelry well worth inspection, was formerly the manor-house of the Grenvilles. Here, history says, died the redoubtable Anthony Payne, who stood 7 ft. 4 ins. in his stockings. He was body-servant to Sir Bevill Grenville. When he died the floor had to be cut away to get the coffin out. In Truro Museum there is a full-length, life-sized portrait of Anthony Payne, painted by Sir Godfrey Kneller in 1680. Stratton will ever be famous for the **Battle of Stamford Hill.** On the wall of the Tree Inn is a tablet brought here from the former monument on the site of the battle. The inscription runs—

"In this place ye army of ye Rebells under ye command of ye Earl of

Stamford receiued a signal overthrow by ye valor of Sir Bevill Grenville and ye Cornish army on Tuesday, ye 16th of May, 1643."

The forces of the Parliament (4,000), entrenched on a neighbouring hill (curiously enough called by the name of the defeated commander), were attacked by the Royalists under Sir Ralph Hopton and Sir Bevill Grenville. The fight raged for ten hours and was all but a victory for the Parliamentarians, but "ye valor of ye Cornish army" prevailed, and victory rested with the King's forces.

Stamford Hill is close to Stratton. Turn up the new Bude road at the south end of the town, turning right, that is, after crossing the bridge, and where the road sweeps to the left turn up a lane to the right ("No through road") with charming views over Stratton. Follow this lane as it climbs Stamford Hill, at the top of which, about a mile from Stratton, and just beyond Bevill house, a gate and stile on the right give access to the pathway. The entrenchment has been pierced to form a sort of gateway, over the top of which is an old pinnacle from Poughill church tower, which was struck down by lightning in the seventeenth century and re-erected here. It is possible to walk nearly all round the grass-grown earthwork, with fine views on every side.

The walk may be continued to **Poughill** by following the road down hill, past the entrenchment, and taking either a narrow lane on the left at the foot of the hill or the first turning on the left, about half a mile farther on. The narrow lane emerges in Poughill a short distance above the church.

II. TO POUGHILL

Either in conjunction with Stratton and Stamford Hill (as above) or as a separate excursion from Bude. The road is that going north from the Post Office, across the golf links and past the Methodist Church at Flexbury Park.

Poughill (pronounced *Poffil*), the ancient *Pochehille*, a mile north of Bude, is, with its thatched *Pudner's Cottage*, one of the prettiest villages around.

Its pleasantly-placed old **Church** (St. Olaf, King and Martyr: *Sundays* 11 and 6), has fine carved woodwork on roof and pews. The foundation is of Norman date, and the bowl of the font beside the south door is of the Norman-Transitional period. The main building and tower are late fourteenth-century. The east window dates from about 1450. The church is famous for its frescoes (*c.* 1470), vividly recoloured in 1894, showing St. Christopher, on the north and south walls. The lock on the old south door is 1 ft. 11 ins. long. The carved bench-ends include a series of emblems of the Crucifixion. The roof is beautifully carved and on the north wall is the copy of Charles I's Letter of Thanks. Some old tombslabs will be noticed in the north aisle, and the church, like most of those in the neighbourhood, contains the Royal Arms, in this case of raised coloured plaster, and dated 1655.

For a circular walk, the return may be made by way of Northcott Mouth and the cliffs. A better alternative is to combine Poughill with a visit to the site of the Battle of Stamford Hill, view the memorial, descend to Stratton, and regain Bude by the footpath. To reach the Memorial from Poughill, ascend the road past the church and either turn right ("to Stratton") at the cross-roads in about half a mile or, about 300 yards above the church, take a lane on the right which leads to the Stratton road near the foot of Stamford Hill. The obelisk stands back a little from the east side of the road beside Bevill House (with white gate) about a mile north of Stratton.

III. TO LAUNCELLS

When at Stratton a pleasant extension of a drive or walk is to **Launcells**, a mile or so farther east. Motorists should follow the Holsworthy road for about a mile. A lane will then be noticed on the left, leading to Launcells, with full directions for finding the church and leaving cars. From this lane another, narrower, lane on the left leads down to the very pretty little valley, tree-embowered and watered by a small stream, in which nestles Launcells church.

A more attractive route leaves Stratton by the road skirting the south side of the churchyard. Disregard left-hand turnings and follow the narrow road as it falls and rises to a farm bearing a notice indicating the path "to the church". Motorists should continue to follow the lane for another quarter of a mile, when on the right will be found a lane also leading "to the church". This lane is that mentioned above as turning out of the Holsworthy Road; the church is reached by a by-lane on the right, and by turning to the right on regaining the main road Stratton will be reached in a mile.

The delightfully situated **Church**, of Launcells (Sundays at 8 a.m., 11 a.m., 6.30 p.m.) is on the site of a Celtic monastery. Dedicated to St. Swithin in 1321, it was reconstructed in the fifteenth century, as were so many other churches in the wave of religious fervour following the Black Death. The church is always open. Note the fine bench-ends, the chancel floor of fifteenth-century Barnstaple encaustic tiles, the early Norman double-cable font, probably made by Saxon workmen, the beautiful plain old crown hand-made glass

Tintagel Castle

Boscastle Harbour

The Breakwater, Bude

Crooklets Beach, Bude

in leaded rectangular panes and the monument (with effigy) to Sir John Chamond, 1624. There are evidences of several wall paintings underneath the whitewash. The absence of a separate chancel, the plain curved altar-rail and the wide spaced pillars, polyphant on the south and granite on the north, contribute to a dignified and impressive simplicity which helps to make Launcells one of the most beautiful churches in the district.

There are several old tombstones, including one which is used as a step to the south porch. **St. Swithin's Holy Well** is on the right at the approach to the car park.

The manor of **Launcells** was held by Robert de Montaine, Earl of Cornwall, half-brother to William the Conqueror.

To return to Bude, go through the gate at the back of the church and across the fields, and turn to the left on reaching the road, which soon leads to Stratton. Go up the lane opposite the church porch. At the top turn to left and on right will shortly be found a track and path leading south-eastward, above the woods, to the Holsworthy Road (buses to Bude pass this point) about a mile short of Red Post.

IV. TO WIDEMOUTH AND MILLOOK

There is a bus service to Widemouth for Wanson Mouth and Millook, while Millook is under 2 miles from Treskinnick Cross on the frequent Camelford service route. An excellent motor road leaves Bude beside the Falcon Hotel, pleasantly overlooking the Canal (*see* our plan), passes through Widemouth and continues to Wanson Mouth, from which it is narrow and steep, though quite passable, to Millook.

Widemouth (pronounced *Widmouth*) sands lie due south of Bude, and are enclosed by fine cliffs. For a cliff walk of about three and a half miles from Bude, climb Compass Hill, beyond the Canal, and continue by the cliff-path past the steep escarpment of Efford Ditch (p. 124), gradually descending to the wide expanse of Widemouth sands, backed by the rugged headland of Dizzard Point. From the heights, glorious sea and land views are obtained. The cliffs from Widemouth Bay Garage to the Breakwater, Bude, have been preserved for the public by the local authority, the portion from Upton to the Breakwater being a generous lease from the late Sir Francis Ackland, M.P.

Widemouth Bay is noted for its fine stretch of sand, and some people ride or walk over from Bude purposely to bathe there. Care must be taken to choose a suitable time, allowing for the distance. There are places where teas can be obtained, and a parking ground in connection with the large café on the beach from which malibou and surf-boards may be hired. The one-time Salthouse—a quaint old place with a bell-shaped chimney —stands lonely on the low cliff at the Bude end of the bay. A notable feature of the bay is the *Black Rock*, where the wrecker Featherstone was condemned to make ropes of sand. Wide-mouth Bay, with shops and a post office, caravan sites and chalets, is gaining in popularity.

From Widemouth the coast road climbs steeply past **Wanson Mouth,** and in places is difficult, but the views are magnificent, and all around are broom, gorse and heather.

Most motorists do not take their cars down to Millook, but park them at the top of the hill—for the descent is steep, 1 in 3, and the lane rather narrow. The road climbing out on the far side of the combe is quite as formidable, but practically all the combes along the coast are similar, and motorists quickly become inured to them. In fact, though great care is necessary, it is more on account of the chance of meeting other cars than because of the dangers of gradient. **Millook** is at the opening of the Trebarfoote Combe, a beautifully-wooded glen that is another favourite spot for picnics. The beach is stony, but the finely contorted cliffs are interesting. It is rather a long walk from Bude to Millook (4⅛ miles each way), and most people, other than motorists, take the bus along the main Camelford road to Bangors Cross. The way is then down a lane past the churchyard, through Trevissick farmyard and Higher Penhalt, and by a stony track to the coast road.

V. A CANAL WALK

An unfrequented and pleasant summer-time walk is along the tow-path of the old Canal. Take the tow-path by the bridge near the Falcon Hotel and continue on by Roddsbridge (boats get up as far as this) and then to Hele Bridge. From this point, the path across the road has become so overgrown that it no longer really exists. Nevertheless, it is an enjoyable and enter-taining excursion to make if only to watch the antics of the rowing boats or to spot the wildflowers growing by the side of the canal.

VI. TO MARHAMCHURCH

This village, with its interesting church, can be reached by road or by way of the Canal path to Hele Bridge, and straight up the hill. A pleasant approach from Hele Bridge is by way of a lane closely following the Neet river as it flows down from Stratton, and then the canal incline. It is a fascinating village, giving a stimulating impression of space, the church standing at the back of a wide square flanked by thatched and colour-washed cottages.

Probably the most novel feature of church and village life which attracts hundreds of visitors each year is the festival known as Marhamchurch Revel. It falls on the Sunday following the 12th August (the Feast of St. Marwenne) and dates from medieval times. The schoolchildren elect a "Queen of the Revel" who is crowned by "Father Time" on the site of the hermitage. Riding on a white horse and followed by attendants, she then leads the procession through the village to the Revel Field where the festivities commence.

The Church, built on the site of an earlier building of the thirteenth century, has a splendid embattled tower. The interior was carefully restored in 1907. The pulpit, richly carved, dates from the time of Charles II; the memorials date from 1581. Note the fine square font and rare four-holed cresset stone, also the fine Delabole slate floor of packed square slates set on end. According to legend a Welsh princess named Marwenne or Marvenna, established her cell in A.D. 500 at Marhamchurch near a well over which the War Memorial now stands. The community grew up around the church. In the fifteenth century an anchoress named Cecelia Moyes occupied a hut attached to the north wall of the sanctuary (the church was cruciform in those days) and the window in the wall through which she used to watch the service and take her communion is now embodied in a small window at the west end of the north aisle. The churchyard commands wide views.

VII. TO KILKHAMPTON

Kilkhampton (6 miles; *London Inn*) is generally reached from Bude by the main road *via* Stratton (bus services). All the coaches *en route* to Hartland and Clovelly pass through, and some wait to give opportunity for an inspection of the fine old church. Kilkhampton is an attractive village healthily placed

nearly 600 feet above sea-level. The tall tower of its church is conspicuous over a wide area.

The Church (services, 8, 11, 6) is mainly Perpendicular, with some striking remains of Norman work, and has been restored in recent years. The stained-glass windows, mostly memorials, are worthy of special notice. On the porch are the arms of John Grenville, Rector, with the date 1567 and the words "Porta Celi". This is the date of the rebuilding of the porch. The church itself was rebuilt in the late fifteenth or early sixteenth centuries. The doorway is a rich specimen of late Norman work, with zigzag ornamentation and heads exactly similar to the porch at Morwenstow (*see* p. 135 for Hawker's interpretation of this design). This doorway deserves careful examination. But it is the carved woodwork which attracts most admiration. Every bench-end is carved in oak black with age, the subjects being emblems of the Passion, initials, and a few grotesques. The decoration of the roofs, especially in the chancel, is also extremely beautiful. The organ is of interest and contains much eighteenth-century pipework. It has a keyboard on which the natural keys are black and the sharps and flats white. It has recently been rebuilt, with a modern console added, but with the incorporation of the ancient keyboard. In the south chapel is a memorial, erected to Sir Bevill Grenville, the victor of Stamford Hill. He met his death shortly afterwards at the Battle of Lansdown, near Bath.

The tower arch at the west end is of lofty proportions. A screen, dating from the restoration of 1860, extends right across the church, with north and south choir screens.

Kilkhampton to Morwenstow.—The most picturesque road route is *via* Stibb and the Combe Valley. The following cross-country route may appear intricate, but is easily followed by walkers, and motorists who do not mind a rough road. Turn to left along narrow road just past church. Road leads down into a valley, passing some cottages on left. In about a mile the road bears to the right, and crosses a small stream. About thirty yards beyond, another stream is crossed by a stone bridge. Ascend the hill; at the top turn to left (signpost for Woodford), and take second turning on right, also marked Woodford, the one to the left leading to Combe Valley by Lee Barton Farm. Now descend and cross a magnificently wooded valley with a small stream; this is the northern arm of **Combe Valley** (*see* below). Both the descent and the ascent on the other side are steep and trying. At the top of the hill is the hamlet of **Woodford**. Take the road bearing round to the right (no signpost, but hamlet is on left), for a mile (passing a lane on the right) and reach Woodford Cross with a signpost. Turn to left, and in a dozen yards take lane on right. It soon joins a main road, and another signpost indicates the road to Morwenstow.

VIII. TO COMBE VALLEY

Road Route *via* Poughill, turning left about half a mile beyond church, and left again at Stibb, about 2 miles farther. The road down into the Combe is steep (1 in 7) and winding, but the woods are delightful.

Walker's Route, 4 miles north of Bude. The road *via* Poughill is available, but for walkers there is the more interesting though arduous route by the cliffs, with a very fine panorama of sea and cliffs on the one hand and pleasantly wooded country on the other. The way is a succession of ups and downs, and several inland detours are necessary. Those who do not wish to go right down to the mouth of the combe should bear off obliquely rightward by a path which leads towards Stibb.

The **Combe Valley** is a vast depression, with steep hills, thickly wooded, and a stream flowing out to sea. A good point from which to see the valley is about half a mile inland, where it divides, giving a beautiful double view. Another lovely scene—the meeting of the valleys by the mill, and on towards the sea—is opened up along the steep road to Morwenstow. Further along the road is a picturesque Mill with a collection of relics of the past. It is set in the midst of semitropical vegetation, while from the little bridge the loveliest pictures of ferns and flowers are seen mirrored in the pools. There is a car park at the Mill, and a road right down to the beach, which has good sands.

Combe Cottage is of interest on account of its connection with that remarkable personality "Hawker of Morwenstow". Here he spent his honeymoon; here he personated a ghost, to the bewilderment of Sir William

Call and his brother, and here he wrote the rousing ballad "And Shall Trelawney Die?"

A good round may be completed by walking to **Kilkhampton** (3 miles up the valley), and returning to Bude (5 miles from Kilkhampton taking the *old* direct road at the proper signpost 1½ miles southward) *via* Stratton, either by bus or on foot. The simplest route is the road *via* Stibb, but infinitely preferable is the road from the hamlet of Combe, between the two valleys, ascending towards Lee, until after the turning for Woodford is passed. Turn right down the lane to Kilkhampton as described the reverse way above. Or walk right up the valley through the woods emerging on to the Kilkhampton Lane through Burridge Farm.

The ancient home of the Grenvilles, **Stowe House**, mentioned by Charles Kingsley in *Westward Ho!* stood nearly a mile inland on the southern side of Combe Valley. Only the site and foundations remain in a field near the farm, for the mansion was destroyed about 1739; but those who pass Stowe Barton will ask themselves whether the great wall facing the road formed part of it or its outbuildings. It was in 1680 that the Earl of Bath—Sir Bevill's son—pulled down the greater part of old Stowe and erected in its place a wonderful structure described by Kingsley as "a huge Palladian pile bedizened with every monstrosity of bad taste". By 1712 Lord Bath and his male heirs were dead, and the title extinct. In 1739 the place was pulled down. The carved cedarwood of the chapel went to Stowe, Bucks; the staircase to Prideaux Place, Padstow: and the rest was scattered in various parts.

IX. TO MORWENSTOW

Road Route.—To Combe Valley as above. Cross stream and ascend farther side of combe (avoiding road inland, to the right) by a gradient of 1 in 7. Run northward for just over 2 miles, to cross-roads whence the left-hand turn leads in half a mile to the Green, where are the *Bush Inn*, some tea gardens and a few cottages. At far end of green turn down to right and through gateway and Morwenstow Church will soon appear on left.

About midway between Combe Valley and Morwenstow is **Stanbury Mouth**, with a sandy beach offering tempting bathing and picnicking.

Walkers who are prepared for a strenuous but enjoyable tramp of about 7½ miles should proceed as directed on p. 133 to the mouth of the Combe Valley, thence follow the road to Stanbury cross-roads, thence left to the beach and by the cliff path to Morwenstow.

Morwenstow lies in a secluded combe on the coast, approximately half-way between Bude and Hartland. A more delightfully secluded spot it would be difficult to imagine. Church and a house stand on the south side of a deep combe, with no other building in sight but the adjacent farm. Across the valley the hillside is aflame with wild flowers, and westward a wedge of intense blue marks where the coast opens to the sea. The

place achieved fame on account of that eccentric genius R. S. Hawker, who was so long Vicar of Morwenstow. The place is becoming increasingly popular among lovers of quiet holidays in healthy and beautiful surroundings.

The **Church**, dedicated to St. John the Baptist, is one of the most interesting in Cornwall. Its ancient foundation is borne out by the record of the endowment. "The striking point of this ancient document is that whereas the date of the endowment is 1296, the church is therein referred to by name as an old and well-known structure. To such a remote era, therefore, we must assign the Norman relics of antiquity which still survive."

Here it was that Robert Stephen Hawker, the learned theologian, the eccentric poet, lived, preached and worked from 1834 to 1875. The porch has numerous points of interest besides the fine Norman doorway. This and the three arches on the north side are said to be the remains of the former church, which in its first form had been dedicated about the year 875, and later enlarged. The pillars of cliffstone are considered to be the finest in Cornwall. Hawker had a wonderful knack of reading significance into the smallest detail of his church. Baring-Gould, in *The Vicar of Morwenstow*, mentions—

"When I first visited the church, I exclaimed at the beauty of the zigzag moulding. 'Zigzag! zigzag!' echoed the vicar, scornfully,' do you not see that it is near the font that this ornament occurs? It is the ripple of the lake of Gennesareth, the spirit breathing upon the waters of baptism. Look without the church—there is the restless old ocean thundering with all his waves, you can hear the roar from here. Look within—all is calm; there plays over the baptismal pool only the Dove who fans it into ripples with His healing wings.'"

The same zigzag moulding over the door will be noticed at

Kilkhampton and at one or two other Cornish churches. Hawker's interpretation is beautiful and poetic.

The font, nearly a thousand years old, is irregular and ornamented with a roughly tooled cable pattern. It is remarkable in having no lead lining. Through the centuries water drawn from St. John's Well by the church has been used in it for baptisms. The bench-ends, dating from 1575, are all finely carved; their various devices and inscriptions are worth careful examination. The graceful screen is mostly modern work, but it incorporates some of the wonderfully-carved original screen erected in 1575. The rood was erected by public subscription in 1934 in memory of Robert Hawker, and the screen restored by Kathleen Martyn in memory of her parents. The fresco on the north chancel wall was discovered in 1884. The entrance door to the nave is of fine Norman work in three orders, but defaced by the removal of the outer to form the arch of the sixteenth-century porch. Note the heads projecting in the spandrels of the arches. There is a very beautiful window, erected in 1904, to the famous Vicar's memory, embodying scenes and legends commemorated in his verse. In addition, various relics of Hawker are kept in the church. With a profound feeling for village life and religious symbolism, he introduced the celebration of harvest by the festival services now so generally held.

In the churchyard the figure-head of the brig *Caledonia* marks the spot where are buried many of her shipwrecked sailors (1842). An ancient cross stands by the church stile. There is also in the churchyard an altar-tomb to John Manning and Christina, his wife, who died 1601.

The **Vicarage**, built by Hawker, is close to the churchyard. The chimney stacks were built to represent different church towers in miniature: Stratton, Whitstone, North Tamerton (with which places Hawker was associated), and two Oxford towers. The kitchen chimney represents his mother's tomb.

A journey to Morwenstow being for many in the nature of a Hawker pilgrimage, most visitors seek out **Hawker's Hut,** a little shanty on the cliffs to which he would retire to be "alone with his books, his thoughts and with God". To reach the Hut take the path running seaward from the stile at the west end of the churchyard. Pass through a gate and a gateway and on reaching cliff edge turn to left. The Hut is not easily seen, as its timbered roof is topped with earth, and lies just below the path, and a half-obliterated sign is above the roof. The Hut with its stable door—but the cliff-top even more—commands magnificent views up and down the coast.

Hidden from view a short distance inland from Morwenstow Green is **Tonacombe,** probably the best specimen of a fifteenth and sixteenth-century manor-house in the West. *The house is not shown to the public except in rare circumstances and if written permission has first been obtained.*

Walkers and motorists, instead of returning to Bude *via* the Combe Valley, can take the road leading eastward for 3 miles, when the main road, with regular bus service in summer from Clovelly to Bude will be reached.

About 2 miles north of Morwenstow and best reached by the glorious, if arduous, walk along the cliffs, is **Marsland Mouth,** a beautiful combe which, with its stream, over 400 feet below the surrounding hills, divides Cornwall from Devon. Readers of Kingsley's *Westward Ho!* will remember how "the fair Rose of Torridge" carried out at Marsland Mouth the witch's instructions, and how the scheming Jesuits were discomfited.

X. TO MILLOOK, POUNDSTOCK AND WEEK ST. MARY

Millook can be reached, *via* Widemouth and Wanson Mouth, a route already outlined on pp. 129 and 130. Walkers for whom the distance is too great should take the Widemouth Bay bus from Bude and alight at Higher Widemouth corner, then proceed by Wanson Mouth and over Penhalt cliff. Millook, with stream, mill and wooded hillsides, is a charming spot for a picnic.

A mile and a half inland from Millook (cars approach only by A 39), is **Poundstock,** a scattered village, with its church of St. Neot, in a sheltered hollow. Note the Norman holy-water stoup in the porch, the square Transition-Norman font, and the frescoes which are to be removed and restored. The designs, however, are shown framed on near-by window sills. Note also the curious old epitaph on the wall behind the font and the elaborately scrolled slate slab. There are wooden sanctuary lamps and chains dating from pre-Reformation times; also a pre-Reformation statue of St. George. The cornice of the new screen to the Lady Chapel depicts scenes from the legendary story of St. Neot. The pulpit is well carved. The registers date from 1615.

There is a Guildhouse, a beautiful fourteenth-century building just below the church, now used for parochial purposes. Here may be seen the old parish stocks.

Between Poundstock and Wanson Mouth is *St. Neot's Well*. North of the church is a track and path going down to Wanson Farm and thence to Wanson Mouth. The well lies on the right-hand side of this track.

Eastward of Poundstock is Bangor's Cross on the main A39 road and ¾-mile further eastward is **Penfound Manor,** one of the oldest inhabited manors in the country. Built originally in Saxon times it displays some Norman, Elizabethan and Stuart features. It contains interesting period furniture and is *open Easter to September, Mondays to Fridays from 2 p.m. to 6 p.m. Charge.*

From Poundstock, it is about a three-mile walk to Week St. Mary. The route is by the eastward lane at Treskinnick Cross, and the greater part of the way is a succession of steep descents and even steeper ascents. The two valleys crossed, however, are charming, and amply repay the toil of the gradients. Nearing Week St. Mary, walkers will find a footpath on the left leading across fields to the church.

If the three places are to be visited in one expedition, it is better to take the Camelford or Tintagel bus as far as Treskinnick Cross.

Week St. Mary is a typical upland North Cornish village (540 ft. above sea-level), looking far more remote than its accessibility warrants. The wide central square contains a War Memorial Cross of the traditional Celtic type which has been generally adopted in the district. A cattle market is held fortnightly and attracts farmers from far and wide.

The substantial **Church** has traces of Norman and Early English masonry in the walls. In the north aisle, once a chantry of St. John the Baptist, a piscina and a few fragments of an altar remain and

138

the rood-loft stairway may still be seen. The octagonal granite font is Late Perpendicular. The fine tower was built in the sixteenth century by Dame Percyval. The church is principally interesting on account of its carved woodwork, both ancient and modern, notably the aisle roofs, remains of ancient carving by the south door, and the unusual narrow pulpit with linen-fold panels. In 1930 a re-seating scheme was incorporated and the excellent new bench-ends indicate that the traditions of the old craftsmen are still observed in the district.

In a field, still known as Castle Ditch, at the west end of the church are a few earthworks—the remains of a Norman Castle, which, with Manor and Borough, belonged in 1085 to Baron Fitzturold, Lord of Cardinham.

About two miles north-east of Week St. Mary is **Whitstone,** with its ancient but much-restored church of St. Anne, containing a beautiful Norman font. In the churchyard is the *Well of St. Anne,* within a canopied arch, with niche at back. *Hilton Wood Castle* is an ancient earthwork, 14 feet high, and there are two other fine ones at Week St. Mary. The two churches of Whitstone and Week St. Mary look across the valley at each other, but the ground between is densely wooded, watered by innumerable streams and steep-sided, so that a detour round the rim of the basin is necessary. The way is as follows: Go up through Week St. Mary along the Launceston road for rather more than a mile, turning to the left at a cross-road, and again to the left at a signpost for Kilkhampton and Bude.

When Whitstone is reached go through the village and turn left at a sign pointing to the church. From this small road an even narrower lane turns off on the left past the Nonconformist cemetery and leads direct to the churchyard gate. Motorists should not take their cars down here as there is not room to turn.

The name **Bridgerule** arises from the old manor-farm called *Bridge,* which was held by one Rual Abdobed, according to the Domesday entry. The fine old church, dedicated to St. Bridget, was enlarged about 1400. It has been carefully restored and beautified in recent years and is well worth a visit

XI. TO JACOBSTOW, ST. GENNYS AND CRACKINGTON HAVEN

Jacobstow is usually visited by road *en route* to Crackington Haven or Tintagel. The church lies in a wooded hollow the best part of a mile from the main road (*bus route*). It contains a massive Transition-Norman font, finely carved, a medieval altarstone, and a fine Elizabethan Communion table. The holy-water stoups remain. The pulpit is formed from ancient bench-ends. The registers date from 1653.

It is a pleasant walk of four miles from Jacobstow to **Crackington Haven,** a romantic spot, with tremendous cliffs towering on each side. There is a bus service to the Haven. Motorists will find the surface good, but careful driving is needed with the 1 in 6 gradients. On the north is **Pencannow Point** (400 ft.), and on the south **Cambeak** (330 ft.). The scene is wild and impressive—an ideal place for a quiet holiday. Where the stream tumbles down the valley, trees are clustered, and a low oak scrub grows on the hillsides. (*See also* p. 104.)

St. Gennys Church (St. Genesius), (*see also* p. 104) with its low, storm-swept pinnacled tower, can be approached by a steep path up the cliffs or by turning to the left some distance up the road to Wainhouse Corner. It is best taken in on the way down, at the fork of the road following the sign by an old white house. Its situation, with the sheltered vicarage behind and farm buildings facing it on the green, is similar to Morwenstow.

High Cliff (731 ft.) is a mile and a half south of Crackington. A short distance inland **Tresparrett Down** rises to 850 feet. **Dizzard Head,** on the other side of Cleave Strand, north-eastwards towards Bude, is nearly 500 feet above sea-level.

XII. TO HOLSWORTHY

Access.—Nearest station, Okehampton, thence coach. *Road.*—Okehampton and Launceston road through Stratton branches at Holsworthy. Entering from the west a magnificent road sweeps round past the church on the outskirts of the town to avoid the very narrow street to the market.
Golf.—The Holsworthy Golf Club has a course of 9 holes 2 miles out on the Bude road.
Parking.—Free on the Square and on Manor Grounds.

Ten miles eastward of Bude by road is the old market town of **Holsworthy** in Devon. It is hardly of sufficient interest to justify a visit in itself, but may be considered worth breaking a journey for when going to or from Okehampton.

The Church of SS. Peter and Paul, built of the pinkish stone so characteristic of Devon churches, is interesting. A chapel of Norman or even pre-Conquest date stood here in 1130, but it gave place to a church in the Early English style in 1250, traces of Saxon work remaining in the porch and massive Norman pillars in the nave. Additions and alterations were made in 1366. The tall-pinnacled tower dates from about 1450.

Blagdon Wharf, about two miles out of Holsworthy, is the inland end of the Bude Canal, but the commercial days of this waterway are over. Holsworthy, however, is a busy market town, and visitors will find it most interesting on Wednesdays when booths for the sale of all kinds of wares occupy the market-place. Cattle market days are Wednesday and Thursday.

A pleasant short round from Bude is to go to Holsworthy *via* Hele Bridge, Marhamchurch, Bridgerule, as described in previous expeditions, and return along the fine main road to Stratton. On the way back, three miles from Holsworthy, a narrow road to the right at the little stream leads up to Pancrasweek, with the lovely church of St. Pancras commanding the rolling country below. It has a closed hagioscope, very tall tower with arch, plain octagonal font, delicate pillars, and good woodwork in the roofs of church and porch.

XIII. TO HARTLAND BY THE CLIFFS

This is a favourite route for really good walkers, for the scenery is magnificent, and the travelling not really difficult when they get used to the deep combes intersecting the coastline. Those accustomed to walking in flatter counties should avoid making too ambitious a programme. As the crow flies Bude is some 12 miles from Hartland in North Devon, but the going is hard (especially in windy weather) and only really strong walkers should try to cover the whole distance in a day. Morwenstow to Hartland is a very good day's work for the average walker.

The route as far as Combe Mouth and on to Morwenstow has already been indicated (p. 134). From Morwenstow to Hartland Quay is about 9 miles. This is the district of "mouths". They are all along this coast—gorges opening to the sea, with rushing streams running through the bottom between boulders, over rocks, and under the shade of many trees. **Yeol Mouth** is about a mile north of Morwenstow, and between rises **Hennacliff,** towering 450 feet above the sea.

In a short mile after crossing **Marsland Mouth** (p. 137), which divides Devon from Cornwall, **Welcombe Mouth** is reached, with the village of **Welcombe** lying a mile inland on the right, and within the Devon border. Devonians pride themselves not a little on the name of the first Devonshire village after the boundary is crossed. The village is popular with visitors, for whom several good farm-houses in the neighbourhood provide accommodation. The surrounding scenery is very attractive, and those looking for a restful holiday away from railways, with the best of sea and country air, would do well to make a note of this hospitable spot. The little grey church of St. Nectan, with its low tower, is of the twelfth or thirteenth century. It has a beautifully-carved screen, which is reckoned the most important feature of the church, and a Saxon font. Note the holy well outside the churchyard gate. Welcombe folk are supposed to be of different race from those of the surrounding parishes, possibly Spanish. The saying, in describing a brunette, is "dark grained as a Welcombe woman".

Motorists approaching Welcombe Mouth should beware of steep hills and narrow lanes. Meads Hill, for instance, drops suddenly with a gradient of 1 in 5. Walkers going from the Church down to Welcombe Mouth may use the old road dropping past the Holy Well, south-east of the Church.

After a stiff climb from the Mouth the path continues northward on high ground for 4 miles, but in many places the cliff is crumbling and care is necessary. **Embury** (or Henbury) **Beacon,** with the remains of an ancient cliff castle, is passed; then a succession of fine cliffs, ranging from 516 feet at **Mansley Cliff.** Leaving Milford on the right, **Speke's Mill Mouth** is reached in about a mile. Here is a good trout stream, ending in a fine waterfall, which is not actually a cascade, as the water slides over a smooth, slightly sloping face of the cliff into a pool, and then with a smaller fall reaches the sea.

A little distance beyond is **St. Catherine's Tor,** a conical grass-covered cliff, rising close to the path. On the extreme summit were discovered remains of a Roman villa. In another mile the drop down to **Hartland Quay** is reached (*see* p. 145).

Hartland and District

Visitors to Bude who intend to spend a day or two, or even a few hours, in exploring the out-of-the-way but most interesting country round Hartland, have the choice of frequent coach tours in summer. Hartland is also on the Bude–Bideford bus route, the service varying with the season. Good walkers will enjoy the long tramp by the cliff path (*see* pp. 141–142) either to or from Hartland.

The road route is through Stratton and Kilkhampton. About 3 miles north of the latter, the road mounts to the high ground of **Woolley Downs** (730 ft.). About half a mile off the road on the right, in the neighbourhood of West Youlstone and Hardsworthy, and near Woolley Barrows, are to be found, close together, the sources of the rivers *Tamar* and *Torridge*. Five and a half miles from Kilkhampton is the *West Country Inn*, a lonely house in a lonely parish. Here the road forks. The left-hand road, over Bursdon Moor, is the nearest for Stoke and Hartland Quay. The road to the right leads, in 4 miles, to Clovelly Dykes—cross-roads, for Hartland (left-hand), Bideford (right-hand), and Clovelly (ahead).

On a clear day it is worth pausing as Bursdon Moor (742 feet) is breasted just beyond the *West Country Inn*, for the sake of the panorama spread below. In the foreground are the patterned fields of Hartland; beyond is Lundy's lonely isle; beyond again the Welsh coast gleams in the sun and if the day is very clear the Black Mountains will be seen looming beyond, while in the north-west the Irish coast appears faint on the horizon. To the south-west lies North Cornwall stretching to St. Ives; to the north-east, North Devon to Mortehoe; farther round to the east Dunkery and the Exmoor heights; in the south-east the Dartmoor hills.

After a brief rise the left-hand road falls steadily and after innumerable turns reaches **Stoke,** a lovely little village between Hartland Town and Hartland Quay.

St. Nectan's Church

is seen on the skyline from many miles away. The tower, which serves as a daymark for shipping, is 128 feet high, including pinnacles, and contains in the east wall a large figure representing St. Nectan. The Church dates from about 1350, the tower from 1400. The

Norman font, from an earlier church, has some grotesque carving. On the north side of the Church is a Norman doorway. There are numerous memorials dating back to 1619. A modern cross, 15 feet high, stands in the churchyard. Excavations for its erection disclosed the base of a cross and an altar-slab with five crosses. The registers date from 1558. The noble carved and coloured screen extends across the entire width of the church, 45 feet. It dates from the fifteenth century, and is exquisitely carved. It is in nearly perfect condition and, except for some minor repairs, is in its original form.

Over the north porch is the Parvise, sometimes erroneously called the "Pope's Chamber"—a mistake arising from the name of Thos. Pope, last Abbot of Hartland. It is the scene of Hawker's *Cell by the Sea* and contains old panels of the pulpit (now happily cleared of the paint which so long disfigured them) and the parish stocks, a barrel organ which formerly reposed on the chancel screen, and other exhibits of interest. The pulpit panels bear the curious inscription GOD SAVE KINGE JAMES FINES, which is explained as follows: the pulpit was bought in 1609–10 (for 33s. 4d.), but the inscription appears not to have been added until 1625–6, the year of King James's death; thus the word "fines" probably signifies "the late King". In the chancel is a beautifully carved tomb from the chapel at Hartland Abbey, demolished in 1769, which served as a communion table until the erection as a war memorial of a new oak altar and reredos. On the south chantry wall is a good brass. Here, too, are fragments of carved stones and some bench-ends.

On the south side of the church is the grave of John Lane, the London publisher (1854–1925).

The happily-placed mansion of *Hartland Abbey,* close to the church, is built on the site, and incorporates the cloisters of an ancient abbey founded in the twelfth century to replace the college established by Gytha, wife of Earl Godwin, as a thanksoffering to St. Nectan for the preservation of her husband from shipwreck. (*Occasional open days—see local press.*)

Other authorities affirm that Gytha established an abbey and not a college of secular canons. All agree that she built a church also. If Gytha was not the foundress of the Abbey it was probably our Geoffrey, son of Oliver de Dynham, who obtained from Henry II licence to change the college of secular canons into regular canons of the order of St. Augustine, and to found a monastery. The transfer was confirmed by Bartholomew, Bishop of Exeter. Richard I granted to the Abbey the ecclesiastical "Right of Gallows". By various grants Hartland was made opulent. In Edward II's reign the cloisters (which are incorporated into the present building) were built, as appears by an inscription still to be seen, which reads when translated: "The variegated quadrangular cloisters built of marble at the expense of, and in the time and by the skill of, the Abbot John, of Exeter, 1312."

To meet the requirements of the fairly large population of Hartland, it would appear that the present St. Nectan's Church was built about 1350, on the site of the church which had accommodated the saint himself. At the Dissolution the Abbey Church, which stood on the east side of the Abbey, was pulled down. With St. Nectan's close by, it doubtless appeared unnecessary to maintain the Abbey Church, which had probably been in existence over five hundred years. In the year 1545 Henry VIII granted "the site of the priory" to one William Abbott. The old buildings had already shown signs of decay, but they do not appear to have been substantially restored, either by the Abbott family or by the Luttrells, who next held them. In 1703, the property passed by marriage to Paul Orchard who carried out major alterations the following year. The Queen Anne staircase and panelled living-rooms were constructed at this time. In 1769, his son, who bore the same name, reconstructed the main building of the Abbey, incorporating into his building the cloisters and part of the then existing walls and pulling down the Abbey chapel. From Orchard the Abbey descended to his great-nephew, L. W. Buck, and from him to his son, who became Sir George Stucley, Bart. The property is still in the possession of the Stucley family.

The valley in which the Abbey stands is very beautiful. Magnificent woods clothe the sides and at the foot flows a lovely stream.

A mile west of Stoke Church the road comes to the cliff edge, descends by steep and sharp bends, and suddenly reveals, at the water's edge, the outpost of—

Hartland Quay

(*Hartland Quay Hotel*). Cars may park at the top or use the road down to the Quay where is space for parking. Besides the hotel there is a swimming pool but the "Quay" is more a name than a reality. The sea-views are magnificent.

The **Lighthouse** at Hartland Point lies 2 miles due north of Hartland Quay, and can be reached by cliff pathway, or narrow motor road from the main Hartland road. The second gateway near the car park is private, but visitors may pass through to the lighthouse. The lighthouse stands on a plateau below the cliffs, 120 feet above sea-level. The revolving light is visible for nearly 17 miles, and shows 6 flashes every 15 seconds. During fog 3 blasts are given every 90 seconds. *The Lighthouse is open to visitors each week-day, the nearby coastguard station every day.* The cliff scenery here is very grand and impressive. From **Hartland Point** (350 feet high) is gained the finest coast view—both ways—in North Devon. Ptolemy called the Point "The Promontory of Hercules". The rocks off the Point are known as the **Cow and Calf.**

The capital of this remote corner of Devon, the little town of **Hartland** (*King's Arms Hotel*), lies rather more than 2 miles inland from the Quay *via* Stoke and a beautiful road displaying Hartland Abbey to advantage. Once an important borough, Hartland is so no longer. Its charter, dated 1285, has lapsed and the mayor and town council have gone. The Town

Hall has vanished too, and on its site was built, in 1839, St. John's Chapel-of-Ease. Today, though a town by courtesy, Hartland is little more than a sleepy village. But its site is healthy and for coast walks it is an excellent centre, with good bus services to Bude and Bideford.

The potentialities of the whole district for camping are rapidly being realized, while motorists and walkers find good roads and footpaths, glorious scenery and hospitable lodging in this far corner of Devon.

Five miles by road from Hartland Town is delightful—

Clovelly

Clovelly has been truly described as "a place unlike any other in the kingdom". It is intensely conscious of the fact and lives accordingly. The one steep street is sometimes so crowded as to restrict movement up or down to a snails pace. It culminates in a series of wide cobble-paved steps. Flowers bloom all over the place, giant fuchsias, almost wild, quite covering the fronts of some of the tiny cottages.

For a full description of Clovelly and neighbouring districts, see the *Red Guide to Bideford and N.W. Devon*.

Car runs in North Cornwall

For **Road Routes** to the District, *see* p. 6.

A first-class road, remarkably free from steep hills, runs parallel to and at only a few miles' distance from that part of the coast covered in this book—practically the whole north coast of the Duchy. From Hayle north-eastwards this is A30, the London–Penzance road, passing through Camborne, Redruth, Blackwater, Zelah, Mitchell and Fraddon. At Fraddon fork left on to A39 which, beyond St. Columb Major and Wadebridge, continues north-eastwards within a few miles of the sea, until it reaches North Devon.

Many of the secondary roads connecting this main artery with the coastal resorts and villages are very steep and narrow, with sudden, unexpected bends, and the motorist who wishes to explore the coast as thoroughly as possible by car will obtain plenty of practice in gear-changing.

Surfaces, on both main and secondary roads, are generally very good, with a safe top-dressing, and local drivers are both considerate and helpful.

Motoring in Cornwall is very enjoyable. The six or seven hundred miles driving over Cornish roads, with all their variety of gradient and aspect, forms a rich and valuable experience.

ROAD ROUTES IN CORNWALL

The district described in this Guide is divided into almost equal parts by the wide and deep estuary of the Camel and its continuing valley from Wadebridge to Bodmin. For our purposes Newquay is the centre of the area south and west of the Camel; and Bude of the northern sector. The routes immediately following comprise only the longer runs from either centre. Notes on routes to places nearer at hand will be found at the head of the description of the place concerned.

(a) TOURS FROM NEWQUAY

NEWQUAY TO TRURO AND FALMOUTH

Leave Newquay by the Trenance Valley and **Trevemper Bridge** where swing right. The road rises gradually all the way to **Zelah Hill** where it joins the Land's End road, and thence gradually descends to Truro. As the city is approached the Cathedral appears beautifully set among the greenery, and there are fine views down the lovely Truro River.

Motorists who are making the river trip between Truro and Falmouth should turn to the left along Quay Street to the Quay where there is a car park close to the bridge.

A pretty alternative route between Newquay and Truro begins at the end of Narrowcliff Promenade and runs inland to **Quintrel Downs** (A3058) and **Summercourt** (the junction with the Bodmin–Redruth highway). Cross this road and go straight ahead to Brighton Cross, where turn right (A39) for **Ladock,** in the valley of the Tresillian River, which is crossed at **Tresillian Bridge.** The Bridge is interesting as the scene of the final surrender of the Royalists to Parliament in 1646; here the terms of peace were arranged. Truro is entered, about 3 miles farther, over Boscawen Bridge, close to the quay from which the Falmouth motor launches start.

For **Falmouth** (11 miles) leave Truro by Falmouth Road (A39), turning southward from Boscawen Street and up Lemon Street, passing the Lander Memorial column on left. The road is as clear as it is beautiful, the steepest hills being beyond Perranarworthal, after Restronguet Creek is crossed. The road is wide and the surface is equal to any road in the British Isles. At top of succeeding hill (A.A. box) turn left. On reaching the warehouses at Penryn, where the road is exceptionally wide, cross the Penryn river bridge and bear left. Here is obtained the first view of the magnificent Falmouth Harbour, one of the finest in the Commonwealth. Shortly the road forks, the road to the left leading along the Penryn river to the town, pier and harbour; that to the right (Dracena Avenue) to the railway station, Pendennis Point and Castle Drive, the bathing beaches and Falmouth Bay. The road to the left also eventually reaches the station.

Falmouth is built across the base of a promontory which extends south-eastward in a seeming endeavour to close entirely the mouth of Carrick Roads and Falmouth Harbour—a beautiful pool about 4 miles long and often more than a mile broad, contained within wooded, rocky shores, broken here and there by the passage of tributary streams and rivers. Of these the most important is the *Fal*, along which launches ply to Truro.

The town and district are fully described in the *Red Guide to Falmouth*, which also contains maps and plans.

NEWQUAY TO THE LIZARD

One of the best ways is *via* the Trenance Valley and Tre-vemper Bridge to **Truro**, as above. Leave (*via* Lemon Street) by the Falmouth Road (A39). At the cross-roads (A.A. Box) near top of hill, a mile or two beyond Perranarworthal, keep straight ahead on to A394 (Falmouth is shortly seen far below on the left). On reaching the Falmouth–Helston road bear right and almost at once turn off on the left for Mabe and Gweek—B3291. The road first follows the Kennal Valley and then climbs out on to the high downs (there are glorious views throughout this drive). Then comes a long run down to **Gweek,** at the head of Helford River, and on to the Lizard Peninsula.

Coaches generally go *via* Helston and continue straight through to **Lizard Town** (about 37 miles from Newquay), near the most southerly point of the Lizard: steep lanes lead on either hand from this road down to the famous coves on the west and east coasts of the Point. On the right going southward from Dodson's Gap turning are signposts for **Gunwalloe** (motorists should not attempt to drive down to Halzaphron Cove), **Mullion,** and **Kynance** (toll road to top of Cove, 5p. which includes car park fee). **Cadgwith** lies a mile or so off the road to the left just beyond Ruan Minor. The road down is very steep and narrow. **Coverack, Porthoustock** and **St. Keverne** lie away across Goonhilly Downs and are best reached by the south-eastward road from Dodson's Gap.

Returning, the road *via* **Helston** passes within a mile of **Looe Pool,** and from Helston a fair road (B3297) climbs over the moors to **Redruth.** The latter part of the journey although

149

somewhat uninteresting gives fine views of Carn **Brea, St.** Agnes Beacon and the sea. In Redruth turn sharp to the right at the cross-roads, ascend the main street (A30) and go on through the suburb of Mount Ambrose to the turning on the left for **Blackwater** and **Zelah.** Here the outward road is rejoined and Newquay reached *via* Trevemper Bridge. *A round of about 85 miles.*

NEWQUAY TO PENZANCE, ST. IVES, AND LAND'S END

This is one of the finest excursions from Newquay. On the outward journey the coast road is usually followed, the return being made by the Land's End–London highway (A30) running through Hayle, Camborne and Redruth. We can give only the route to and from Land's End; but the motorist who appreciates fine rock scenery should follow some of the minor lanes running down to the south of the peninsula.

Newquay is left by the Trenance Valley and **Trevemper Bridge,** where swing right. At far end of Goonhavern fork right for **Perranporth,** a glimpse soon being caught on the right of the waste of sand-hills among which St. Piran's Church lies hidden. A steep ascent from Perranporth, a 4½ miles run across more open country, and **St. Agnes** is reached where five roads meet. The road to the right leads down to the beautiful **Trevaunance Cove** in half a mile (*Car Park*) and neither this nor the Beacon Drive should be missed while in this district. From St. Agnes the road passes **Porthtowan** with its lofty cliffs and broad sands, then, after passing inland owing to the closing of the coast road at this point, the small resort of **Portreath,** beyond which a steep climb (keep to the right at the top of the hill) leads out on to the heather-clad cliffs bordering the road almost all the way to **Gwithian.** The road passes Deadman's Cove and Hell's Mouth and fine views are obtained of jagged rocks with the waves creaming at their feet.

After sandhills at Gwithian the road turns inland. The right-hand turning opposite the inn in Gwithian meets the Land's End road as it enters **Hayle,** a straggly place with huge towans along the shore. It follows the Hayle River round to the left until, immediately after passing beneath a railway bridge, it swings very sharply to the right again passing under the bridge, and after a short winding course resumes its companionship with the Hayle estuary. About a mile beyond Hayle a road on the left leads to Ludgvan and Penzance, and as the shores of Mount's Bay are approached there is a splendid view of **St. Michael's Mount** to the left.

Visitors making only a brief halt will probably be less interested in **Penzance** as a town than as a view-point. To avoid the busy main road through the town, turn left at Railway Station and then right, round the harbour, past the Swimming Pool and along the front. Well placed on a small promontory overlooking Mount's Bay, it commands views that have been painted times without number. **Newlyn,** beloved by artists, lies a mile or so to the right, looking seaward; to the left St. Michael's Mount rises very beautifully from the floor of the Bay, and beyond, the coast can be followed as it runs southward to form the western buttress of the Lizard promontory.

Penzance itself is full of interest but for its description readers are referred to the *Red Guide to Penzance and West Cornwall.*

Unless the detour round Penzance Harbour is preferred, keep to the road which, just past the station, becomes known as Market Jew Street—the main thoroughfare of the town. At Alverton Bridge turn to the left and in about a quarter of a mile keep to the left again, just after a sharp swing to the right. The direct road is that to the right at Lower Hendra, about 3 miles out from Penzance; gradually rising and then falling and bending first this way, then that, it leads to **Sennen Churchtown** and so to the **Land's End,** some 44 miles from Newquay. The left-hand road at Hendra runs *via* St. Buryan to Treen and then strikes north-west to **Sennen,** passing near some of the finest rock scenery in Cornwall.

Returning, follow the main road till about a mile beyond Sennen Churchtown, when the **St. Just** road is taken. Beyond St. Just there begins a series of windings and twists that will try the patience of the driver and encourage digressions to view the fine cliff scenery of the north coast. Just under 20 miles from the Land's End **St. Ives** comes suddenly into view, and a very steep road leads down into this crowded little town. The charms of St. Ives centre about its Harbour, always interesting with its gulls, its boats and—no less—its boatmen.

A steep climb affording magnificent views across the bay leads from St. Ives to the upper portions of the rising resort of **Carbis Bay.** Then there is a smooth run down to Lelant (sharp turn to right) and pretty wooded roads rejoin A30 bordering the estuary to **Hayle.** From Hayle a broad highway leads in a few miles to **Camborne.** Then comes the busy town of **Redruth,** through which the road descends steeply and ascends the equally steep hill opposite. Just short of Scorrier Station fork left on to A30, passing through **Blackwater,** forking left again at Trevissome, and so to **Perranzabuloe** and **Newquay.** *A round of just over 100 miles.*

NEWQUAY TO TINTAGEL AND BOSCASTLE

Few visitors leave North Cornwall without a visit to King Arthur's Country. The route from Newquay starts by Narrowcliff Promenade, turning inland to **St. Columb Minor** and thence by a pretty road to **St. Columb Major,** high on the hills. Turn left entering town and descend (keep to the right at the fork a hundred yards or so down) along the **Wadebridge** road. At Winnards Perch the road for **Padstow** goes off to the left and a little farther there is a glimpse, on the right, of the *Nine Maidens,* and on the same side there are distant views of the Bodmin Moors, while the tall Gilbert Obelisk marks the position of Cornwall's county town. Farther to the right are the radio masts at Bodmin.

Wadebridge is entered after a long steady descent. *Beware the level crossing at foot of hill.* Cross the Bridge with care and turn immediately to the left, almost at once swinging to the right and climbing along the **Camelford** road. Just before the town is entered take a turning on the left. Bear sharp to the left on crossing the railway and take second road on right for Tintagel.

Those wishing also to see **Trebarwith Strand** *en route* for Tintagel pass down a pretty, deep valley, its sides littered with quarry debris and thickly clothed with bracken and heather. The road narrows considerably at several points as it runs between the stone walls, and there are one or two rather sharp turns, but the gradient is quite moderate down to the little hotel at Trebarwith Strand.

Returning up the valley, take the first turn on the left, crossing the head of the valley and ascending steeply through Trewarmett. (Good views backward over Trebarwith.) **Tintagel** is a mile or so farther—about 30 miles from Newquay.

The return from Boscastle is usually made by way of the road passing near the *Wellington Hotel* and climbing the south side of the valley, above the village, and leading to **Camelford** direct; but it is sometimes extended by following the road climbing out of Boscastle by the northern side of the valley, turning southward again at **Tresparrett** (inn) for the Bude–Camelford road. Tresparrett lies high, and the last mile or so of the road up from Boscastle provides very extensive views.

NEWQUAY TO PADSTOW VIA COAST ROAD

One of the most attractive routes from which to enjoy the magnificent coastal scenery of North Cornwall, and to explore the many lovely coves and beaches *en route*, is to travel the Newquay to Padstow coast road. The route is hilly, sometimes with sudden bends, and calls for careful driving.

Starting from Newquay Station, take the St. Columb road (A392) along the front, but leave it shortly after turning inland (first main turning on left and well-signposted) for **St. Columb Porth;** a small but very pleasant and increasingly popular resort with excellent sands. Continue up Watergate Road (B3276) and from the summit and during the steep descent to **Watergate Bay** (low gear advised) fine views are obtained. If low tide a stop of half an hour is suggested here for a stroll along the beach from which the wild beauty of the rugged cliffs can be admired from below.

Continue up the sharp ascent by side of hotel and at the hamlet of Trevarrion bear left to rejoin B3276. The road now descends increasingly steeply to **Mawgan Porth.** Shortly before reaching sea-level a sudden and awkward bend to right needs care and attention. Here is a beautiful sandy bay with towering headlands with several houses and bungalows sprinkled about,

153

and refreshment rooms and a filling station. Disregard the turning to right and make the steep climb up to Trenance, taking the sharp turn to the left near top of hill. In about 1¼ miles notices offer the visitor the use of a car park (refreshments obtainable) from which a short walk enables him to view the noble expanse of **Bedruthan Steps.** Continuing, the pretty sandy cove at **Porthcothan Beach** comes into view in 2½ miles.

In a few hundred yards beyond, leave B3276 and turn left, continuing for a mile and a half to reach **Treyarnon Sands** (car park and refreshments at Hotel). Return to B3276 by avoiding the right-hand turn (back to Porthcothan) and, instead, turn left at junction. Continue for three-quarters of a mile and, just before reaching St. Merryn, turn left again for **Harlyn Bay** with its sandy beach and rocky headlands. Continue forward and in 1 mile regain B3276 about half a mile north-east of St. Merryn.

In another quarter of a mile turn left again for **Trevone,** a rising little resort with increasing amenities, hotel and a few shops. Both here and at Harlyn Bay, the cliffs are not so high or so wild and rugged as in other parts of North Cornwall, but the scenery is very attractive nevertheless. From Trevone the same route must be retraced to B3276, where turn left.

In 1¼ miles the ancient and picturesque port of **Padstow** is reached by a steep and awkward descent (car park on North or South Quay). Distance from Newquay about 16 miles.

The return journey can well be made over most of the same route, but passing through St. Merryn (*see* p. 76) and omitting the diversions to Trevone, Harlyn, Treyarnon and Porthcothan—a distance of 12 miles or approximately 25–30 for the round trip out and back from Newquay.

NEWQUAY TO BUDE

To Camelford as in the Boscastle–Tintagel excursion, but instead of turning off on left keep straight on through town (a sharp dip and rise) and thence by a good undulating road through pretty, open country to **Bude,** 43 miles.

For an interesting alternative return route (longer than the foregoing by some 20 miles), turn up Stratton Road in Bude and go through ancient and picturesque **Stratton** to the sleepy town of **Holsworthy.** Here turn right, descend sharply on leaving town and so by a good undulating road to **Launceston.** This town is approached by a steep ascent from its suburb of Newport; the Bodmin road goes off to the right near the top of the hill. In more than two miles leave the Camelford road on right and strike across the moors—Rough Tor and Brown Willy are seen away to the right, and Dozmary Pool is on the left at Bolventor. In the distance the curious white pyramids marking the china clay pits beyond Bodmin catch the eye, and the tall masts of the wireless station. Descending into **Bodmin,** after a splendid run across the moors, pass the church, bear round to left and then to right through the heart of this busy old town.

From Bodmin continue to follow the main road through pretty little Lanivet, shortly beyond which bear up to the right, past the great wireless station. Beyond Roche Station, road and railway run side by side for nearly three miles and turnings on the right are marked "To Newquay".

NEWQUAY TO FOWEY

The route, with good roads is *via* St. Columb Minor and Major to Roche (*see* p. 52), climbing thence over bleak Hensbarrow Down to **St. Austell,** the busy centre of the china clay industry. Hence the road to Fowey is eastward by St. Blazey Gate and Par.

Another route is along the Bodmin road until a mile or so beyond the wireless station, by Lanivet, where a sharp backward turn to the right near the foot of a hill leads towards St. Austell. Almost immediately leave this road by a left-hand turning which joins the Bodmin–St. Austell road near Lanhydrock House. Here turn to the right, and in about 4 miles take a left-hand road leading to **Fowey** (*foy*) on the south coast of Cornwall, midway between Plymouth and Falmouth. Owing to very narrow, winding and hilly streets, the greatest vigilance is necessary in driving about Fowey. The town and district are described in the *Red Guide to South Cornwall.*

NEWQUAY TO LOOE AND POLPERRO

The first part of this trip is eastward to Bodmin. Go right through the town and at the foot of Fore Street keep to left and bear round to right. Passing round the church turn up to right by the Launceston Road, and in about a quarter of a mile take the Liskeard and Plymouth road, on the right, which soon descends again, and for about 10 miles is extremely pretty, following the Fowey river up the Glynn Valley. Students of place-names can muse over *Doublebois*, the former railway company's version of **Dobwalls,** a village crowning an ascent and heading a turning leading through **Duloe** to the main Polperro–West Looe Road. The Liskeard road, however, descends from Dobwalls, and, after passing through Liskeard, runs above the eastern side of the Looe valley through Morval to **East Looe,** a little over 40 miles from Newquay.

Looe is a flourishing little town situated on both sides of the mouth of a stream, 8 miles, as the crow flies, east of Fowey. *See* the *Red Guide to South Cornwall.*

(b) TOURS FROM BUDE

Road routes to places near at hand will be found at the head of the descriptive notes on other pages. The following are among the more popular of the longer tours.

The country eastward from Hartland is fully described in the *Red Guide to Bideford and North-West Devon*, which contains maps and plans of the towns named.

BUDE TO HARTLAND AND CLOVELLY

Turn eastward up Stratton Road and make for **Stratton.** On approaching the village take the *second* turn down on the right, and in village turn to the left or Stratton may be avoided by taking the new road at the top of the hill just before the town. The road rises and passes through Kilkhampton to the *West Country Inn* (about 12 miles from Bude). Here the direct route to **Stoke** and **Hartland** bears off to the left (*see* p. 143); for Clovelly keep on the right and 2 miles farther, at Baxworthy Corner, turn sharp to the right. A left-hand turn in rather more than a mile leads to **Clovelly Cross,** whence it is a clear run to the large car park at the head of the steep Combe with **Clovelly** at its mouth, 16 miles from Bude.

BUDE TO BIDEFORD AND BARNSTAPLE

To Clovelly Cross (15 miles from Bude), as above, but instead of turning left for Clovelly go straight on past Hobby Lodge. It is almost exactly 10 miles on to Bideford, along a road affording splendid views across Bideford Bay.

The entrance to **Bideford** requires care. Descending Old Town Street turn to the right into Meddon Street, and then, passing the old workhouse building, turn off on right again down Torridge Hill. At the foot of the hill turn sharp to the left and Bideford Bridge will be seen in front. The *car park* is beyond the bridge, by the Quay.

For **Westward Ho!** turn inland from the north end of the Quay by way of Kingsley Road. Northam is reached in little more than a mile, and a sharp and awkward left-hand turn leads out to **Westward Ho!** Straight ahead in Northam leads to pretty little **Appledore,** at the head of the Torridge.

For Barnstaple cross Bideford Bridge, turn sharp to the left and in a few hundred yards go over a steep railway bridge (*caution*). The road now follows the Torridge to **Instow,** giving lovely views across the blue waters to Appledore. On approaching Instow keep to the right and the road is then clear to **Barnstaple.**

BUDE TO TINTAGEL, BOSCASTLE, ETC.

Bude is left by the Camelford road. Beware the sharp double turn under the railway at **Helebridge.** About $1\frac{1}{2}$ miles beyond Wainhouse corner keep to the right, and at **Tresparrett Posts** (inn) keep straight on (the road to the left leads direct to Camelford). Shortly there are splendid views of the coast ahead, and inland a wide panorama is unfolded. Then the road descends, dropping to **Boscastle** fairly steeply about 15 miles from Bude.

For Tintagel cross the bridge and ascend the steep road beyond (hair-pin bend). Near the top of the village turn up to the right. The road is now unmistakable to **Tintagel** (19 miles from Bude), though care should be taken in descending to and climbing from the Rocky Valley (1 in 6 gradients).

From Tintagel it is worth while, time permitting, to return *via* **Trebarwith Strand,** a mile or so southward. Take the road opposite King Arthur's Hall and follow it as it descends steeply from Trewarmett. The valley is crossed by a kind of embankment, at the farther end of which turn sharp left for Camelford; sharp right for Trebarwith. Return up the valley by the same road and continue to Camelford Station, where turn right over the railway. Those requiring **Camelford** turn off to the right at the top of a steep hill at the edge of the town, and then almost at once turn left, down the steep and rather narrow High Street that is apt to be awkwardly full of traffic at times. This runs right through the town to the Bridge, beyond which the road climbs to the high moorland country, rejoining the outward route at Tresparrett. *A round of about 50 miles.*

BUDE TO BODMIN

The best route from Bude is *via* Camelford (*see* above). Keep straight through the town and on to **Wadebridge,** which is entered by a descent with a sharp left turn at the foot. Do not cross the bridge, but continue with the broad river on the right, past Egloshayle, to **Bodmin,** 37 miles from Bude. Beyond Sladesbridge the road becomes hilly, and is in parts beautifully wooded. *Beware level crossing at Dunmere.*

BUDE TO PADSTOW AND NEWQUAY

From Bude go *via* Camelford to Wadebridge, as in the excursion to Bodmin. On descending into the town and turning to the left, look out for the turning on the right crossing the Bridge, and at the farther end of the Bridge beware of the level crossing. Hence the road goes straight up through **Wadebridge** and on to **St. Columb Major** (one way street), where at the end of the town turn right for **Newquay.**

For **Padstow,** however, take the right-hand turn about 2 miles out of Wadebridge. The road drops steeply into Padstow, with awkward bends at the foot of the hill.

Index

Where more than one reference is given, the first is the principal.

INDEX